OECD Public Governance Reviews

Public Procurement in Chile

POLICY OPTIONS FOR EFFICIENT AND INCLUSIVE FRAMEWORK AGREEMENTS

This document was approved by the Public Governance Committee on 23 December 2016 and prepared for publication by the OECD Secretariat.

This document and any map included herein are without prejudice to the status of or sovereignty over any territory, to the delimitation of international frontiers and boundaries and to the name of any territory, city or area.

Please cite this publication as:
© OECD (2017), *Public Procurement in Chile: Policy Options for Efficient and Inclusive Framework Agreements*, OECD Public Governance Reviews, OECD Publishing, Paris.
http://dx.doi.org/10.1787/9789264275188-en

ISBN 978-92-64-27517-1 (print)
ISBN 978-92-64-27518-8 (PDF)

Series: OECD Public Governance Reviews
ISSN 2219-0406 (print)
ISSN 2219-0414 (online)

The statistical data for Israel are supplied by and under the responsibility of the relevant Israeli authorities. The use of such data by the OECD is without prejudice to the status of the Golan Heights, East Jerusalem and Israeli settlements in the West Bank under the terms of international law.

Photo credits: Cover © magic pictures/Shutterstock.com.

Corrigenda to OECD publications may be found on line at: *www.oecd.org/about/publishing/corrigenda.htm*.

Foreword

Governments across OECD countries are seeking to make public service delivery more efficient and cost-effective, largely because of budgetary constraints but also to respond to growing expectations from citizens. In exploring different policy options, they are finding that technical policy instruments, such as procurement contracting tools, can also be levers for change. This report looks at framework agreements in the procurement processes in Chile.

The Government Programme of Chile for the period 2014-2018 defined an ambitious set of economic, political and social reforms, including measures to improve public service delivery. These measures involved changes to public procurement to make it more sustainable and efficient. Representing almost one-third of government expenditure, public procurement significantly impacts on the delivery of public services, either directly with the provision of infrastructure, healthcare services or educational facilities, for example, or indirectly by generating business opportunities for the private sector. Strategic public procurement, by streamlining and rationalising processes, supports public sector transformation and productivity growth and shapes the private sector's contribution to public service delivery. It also allows government to evaluate policy efficiency in an area that has a direct economic impact.

Framework agreements are contracts between one or more public contracting authorities and one or more suppliers, establishing general terms governing purchase orders to be awarded during the agreement's term. Largely implemented in countries around the world, they can be used to aggregate public demand and streamline procurement processes. One of the first Latin American countries to implement framework agreements, Chile progressively expanded their use by both the central government and municipalities. Chile's central purchasing body, the Directorate of Government Procurement and Contracting of Chile (also known as ChileCompra), has developed framework agreements in a growing number of product categories. It also developed an electronic marketplace where purchase orders can be processed by contracting authorities. The implementation and development of this instrument proved to be highly successful. The electronic catalog of framework agreements called ChileCompra Express is the largest online store in the country and is almost equivalent to all private electronic commerce in Chile. Yet, in pursuing the government's objective to promote an inclusive public procurement system, ChileCompra has been overwhelmed by the steady increase of the number of awarded suppliers and the exponential growth of contract management activities. These trends called into question both the sustainability and the efficiency of the current system.

In an attempt to optimise the system, ChileCompra is revising the design and functioning of framework agreements, and has asked the OECD to assist in this undertaking, based on its 2015 Recommendation on Public Procurement as well international good practices and insights in implementing and managing framework agreements.

Focusing on framework agreements, this report evaluates the impact that broader policy objectives such as inclusiveness have had on the performance of Chile's procurement. It recommends strategic choices for improving ChileCompra's framework agreement system, and suggests ways to streamline processes, improve the effectiveness of the system and increase efficiencies while promoting inclusiveness.

The report also presents key results from a comprehensive benchmarking survey on framework agreements conducted in the beginning of 2016. Current practices in different jurisdictions provided background evidence and data for the analysis.

This report is part of OECD's work to help governments at all levels design and implement strategic, evidence-based and effective policies to strengthen public governance.

Rolf Alter
Director, Public Governance Directorate.

Acknowledgements

Under the direction of Rolf Alter, OECD Director for Public Governance and Territorial Development, and supervision of János Bertók, Head of the Public Sector Integrity Division, this review was led by Matthieu Cahen, Senior Policy Analyst under the guidance of Paulo Magina, Head of the Procurement Unit. Kenza Khachani and Minjoo Son, Policy Analysts, also drafted sections of the report. Editorial assistance was provided by Thibaut Gigou, Laura McDonald. Anaisa Goncalves, Pauline Alexandrov and Alpha Zambou provided administrative assistance.

The OECD expresses its gratitude to ChileCompra for its fruitful co-operation, the invitation to benchmark the design, use and management of their collaborative procurement instruments against international good practices, and for their open dialogue throughout the review process. Under the leadership of Director Trinidad Inostroza Castro, special thanks are offered to the staff of ChileCompra, in particular Guillermo Burr, Head of Research and Business Intelligence Department, Dora Ruiz Madrigal, Head of Framework Agreement Division, Claudio Loyola Castro, Head of Technology and Business Division, Elena Mora, Coórdinator for Intersectoral Networks, and Simón Benito Stuardo Novoa, Project Analyst, for providing supporting information and facilitating interviews with relevant stakeholders during co-ordination of the peer review process. Consuelo Herrera from the Permanent Delegation of Chile to the OECD was instrumental in supporting the OECD in this project.

Special thanks also goes to the lead reviewer, Shayne Gray, Commercial Manager, Ministry of Business, Innovation and Employement, New-Zealand.

The OECD expresses its gratitude to its member countries and the delegates of the Working Party of Leading Practitioners on Public Procurement for having responded to the survey on framework agreements which was pivotal in providing grounds and evidence base to benchmark the use of framework agreements in different contexts, applications and results.

Table of contents

Figures

Tables

Boxes

Executive summary

Efforts to improve procurement procedures, reduce duplication and achieve greater value for money have led to the development across OECD countries of policies promoting the use of collaborative procurement tools and strategies such as centralised purchasing, framework agreements, dynamic purchasing or joint procurement. They are also reflected in the 2015 OECD Council Recommendation on Public Procurement.

A framework agreement is an agreement between one or more contracting authorities and one or more economic operators, the purpose of which is to establish the general terms governing purchase orders to be awarded during a given period. The implementation and development of this instrument proved highly successful and became very popular in Chile. In the last five years the number of purchase orders increased by 150% and the number of transacting suppliers by more than 130%. However, this success also raised questions about the sustainability of the current framework agreement model, as requests for modifications of suppliers' catalogues of products increased by 758% during the same period.

The concept and functioning of framework agreements (*Convenios Marco*) in Chile, is somewhat different from the most commonly admitted principles surrounding the implementation and use of this strategic procurement instrument, as illustrated by the comparison with other OECD country practices.

First and foremost, ChileCompra is one of the few central purchasing bodies (CPBs) that have very few framework agreements that are made with a single supplier. Apart from the framework agreement relating to mandatory health insurance, all other instruments are concluded with multiple suppliers. On average, ChileCompra awards a framework agreement to 185 suppliers out of 248 bids received. This means that almost 70% of the bidders are admitted under framework agreements. Yet, more than 60% of suppliers on average did not receive any purchase orders in 2014, and the top 10 suppliers under each framework agreement accounted for, on average, 71% of the total revenue.

Indeed, the number of suppliers participating in framework agreements signals a different approach towards the use of this instrument, since most OECD countries use this tool to improve efficiency and extract value for money and cost savings from the system by aggregating and consolidating demand, thus reducing the pool of suppliers. Framework agreements in Chile thus more closely resemble other collaborative procurement tools such as dynamic purchasing systems or e-catalogues.

Yet, other aspects of the framework agreements implemented by ChileCompra differ from these alternative solutions. For example, dynamic purchasing systems (DPS) in the European Union qualify suppliers solely based on the attainment of fixed technical requirements. In addition, contrary to framework agreements in Chile, suppliers are allowed to join the existing DPS at any point in time following an open call for tender, and second stage competition is mandatory for all subsequent purchase orders. This type of instrument is significantly different from the functioning of framework agreements in Chile where less than 1% of the purchase orders are subject to second stage competition.

These specificities, high number of awarded suppliers and limited second stage competition, are central to the entire approach of ChileCompra to framework agreements. They are certainly inclusive, offering the private sector broad access to the public procurement market, yet with limitations relating to the effective inclusiveness of the system since the majority of awarded suppliers are not receiving any revenue in a given year. At the same time, the sustainability of the model, both for the public and the private sides, is far from certain.

One of the options ChileCompra could consider is to turn framework agreements into consolidated tools generating economies of scale. This would imply the rationalisation of both demand and supply, but could reduce their inclusiveness. Otherwise, Chile could choose to maintain the existing structure and focus on increasing the sustainability of the system notably by streamlining the operational management of framework agreements, but probably at the expense of efficiency in achieving value for money and savings.

In order to balance the benefits and the aforementioned risks associated with both options, Chile could follow another path: that is, a progressive and targeted implementation of strategic consolidation efforts, such as standardisation of products and aggregation of needs. Benefiting from the experience of other countries, ChileCompra could build upon the hybrid nature of its existing framework agreements system to develop an architecture whereby current inclusive collaborative procurement tools would sit alongside targeted consolidated procurement instruments.

ChileCompra could increase savings by identifying product categories more prone to the development of economies of scale, reducing the pool of suppliers, standardising product categories and strategically allocating the market to suppliers after a competitive process. For product categories with highly heterogeneous demand such as food and perishables, ChileCompra could reinforce the inclusiveness of the corresponding instruments by allowing suppliers to join existing instruments at set entry points. Alongside structured product updates, these efforts would help improve the operational efficiencies of framework agreements.

Chapter 1.

Snapshot of the use of framework agreements in Chile

Since their establishment in 2003, the use of framework agreements in Chile has increased dramatically. More contracting authorities rely on this collaborative procurement instrument, and awarded suppliers have doubled in the last two years. Under the responsibility of Chile's Central Purchasing Body, ChileCompra, the sustainability and efficiency of the system are now at stake, which poses new challenges on how to support and manage the increasing use of this instrument. This chapter provides an overview of the major trends of the existing public procurement system in Chile and highlights the underlying objectives of framework agreements. It also includes the results from a benchmarking exercise across several OECD and non-OECD countries, which uses the responses received from the 2015 OECD Survey on Centralised Framework Agreements.

Chile's approach to framework agreements

According to data published in 2011 (OECD, 2011a), public procurement in Chile accounted for almost 7% of gross domestic product (GDP) in 2008. In 2013, OECD countries spent, on average, 12.1% of GDP on public procurement, translating into an average of 28.4% of the total general government expenditure, compared to an average level of 29.4% in 2009 (OECD, 2015a). Considering the significance of public expenditure, enhancing efficiency, including increasing cost effectiveness, is the primary objective of public procurement.

Collaborative procurement instruments are among the most commonly used tools that procurement officials use to drive efficiency and cost effectiveness. They open the door to streamlined procurement processes, reduced duplication of administrative costs and increased government purchasing power. While different contractual mechanisms are included in this collective approach to public procurement, a framework agreement, albeit with different specificities, is the most routinely adopted instrument by countries.

While framework agreements might be seen as a purely technical instrument applied to public procurement, it conveys principles and skills that contribute to the development of procurement as a strategic function. Demand analysis, responding to user needs and performance assessments provide tangible evidence of procurement efficiencies. Framework agreements directly address the major principles set forth in the 2015 OECD Recommendation on Public Procurement (OECD, 2015b).

The use of framework agreements by some or all procuring entities at the central government level is widespread among OECD countries: 97% of responding countries reported their use in 2012 (OECD, 2012). Furthermore, an increasing number of OECD member countries have implemented central purchasing bodies at the central level in order to aggregate demand and to act as manager of the national system that awards consolidated instruments, including framework agreements (Figure 1.1). In the European Union, framework agreements represented 27% of the number and 42% of the value of all central purchasing contracts during 2008 and 2009 (EC, 2011). The use of collaborative procurement tools represents a shift towards the implementation of strategic procurement.

Figure 1.1. Role of central purchasing bodies

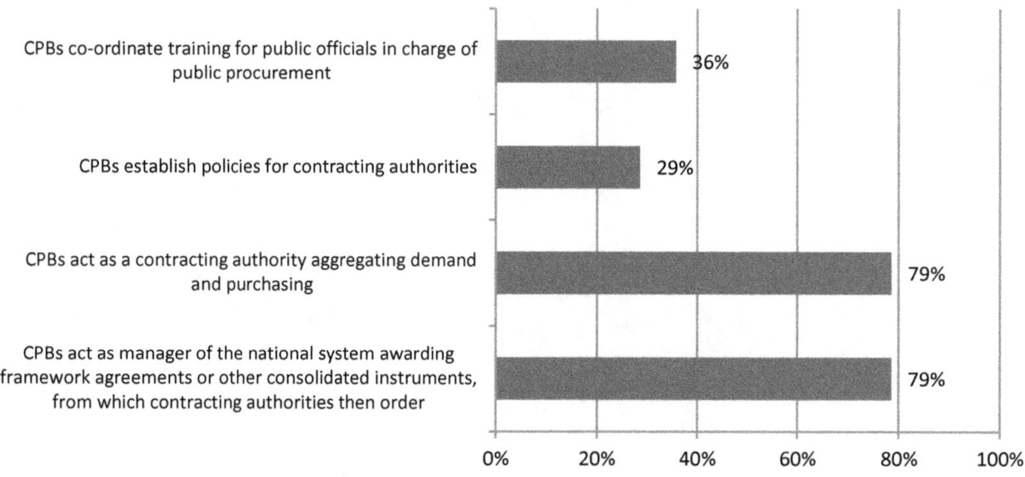

Source: Adapted from OECD (2015a), *Government at a Glance 2015*, OECD Publishing, Paris. http://dx.doi.org/10.1787/gov_glance-2015-en.

The Chilean government programme for 2014-2018 aims to modernise the state to enhance efficiency and innovation. In line with this, the Directorate of Government Procurement and Contracting of Chile, ChileCompra, as the governing body of public procurement and acting as a central purchasing body, is currently reviewing some of its practices, processes, technologies and operation models.

ChileCompra is the central purchasing agency in Chile. Its main duties are: 1) provide support to public entities in carrying out procurement processes; 2) implement, operate and maintain the information system, allowing public entities to conduct online procurement operations; 3) manage the registry of suppliers; 4) purchase goods and services on behalf of one or more public entities; and 5) implement and manage framework agreements. ChileCompra's role is therefore twofold: developing procurement policies of the country, and implementing collaborative procurement instruments for the benefit of contracting authorities.

Framework agreements (*Convenio Marcos*) have been instituted in Chile since 2003. The Law n° 19 886 on Public procurement[1] states that ChileCompra is responsible for implementing and managing this type of agreement. A bylaw[2] further details obligations of the public entities using framework agreements.

With the mandate and responsibility for managing framework agreements, ChileCompra developed an electronic platform, ChileCompra Express, for accessing all goods and services available for purchase by public entities.

In 2014, around 850 public entities procured goods and services through the electronic platform administered by ChileCompra. In the same year, a total of 810 434 purchase orders of approximately USD 1.8 billion were made on ChileCompra, and such transactions, in terms of accumulated value since being established, amounted approximately to 4.7 million of purchase orders for USD 10.5 billion. In particular, the use of framework agreements by public entities has experienced exponential growth over the last years, as Figure 1.2 shows.

Figure 1.2 Uptake of framework agreements by contracting authorities

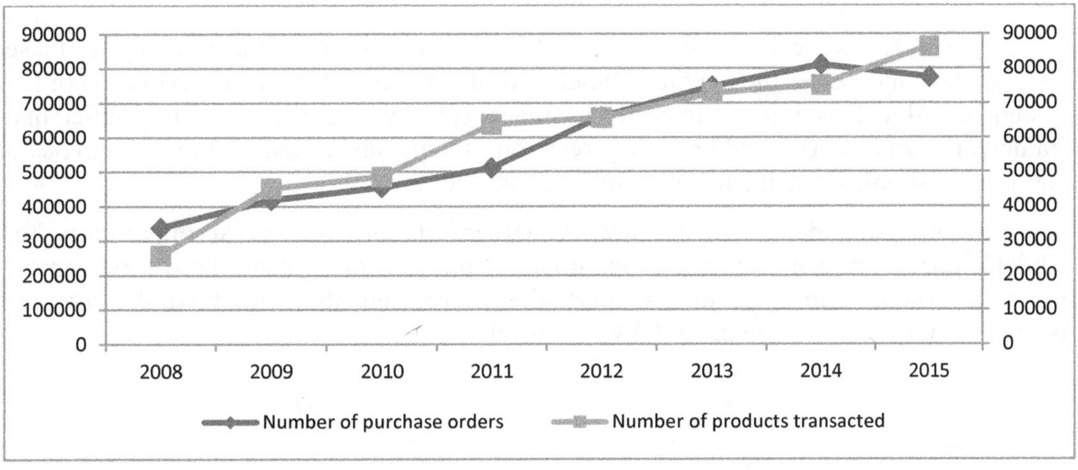

Source: Information provided by ChileCompra.

ChileCompra Express allows public entities to purchase goods and services available in the framework agreements. The electronic platform also allows suppliers to modify their offerings. Changes to products specifications and prices submitted by suppliers are then assessed by ChileCompra and incorporated into the platform, if deemed appropriate.

Figure 1.3 Uptake of framework agreements by suppliers

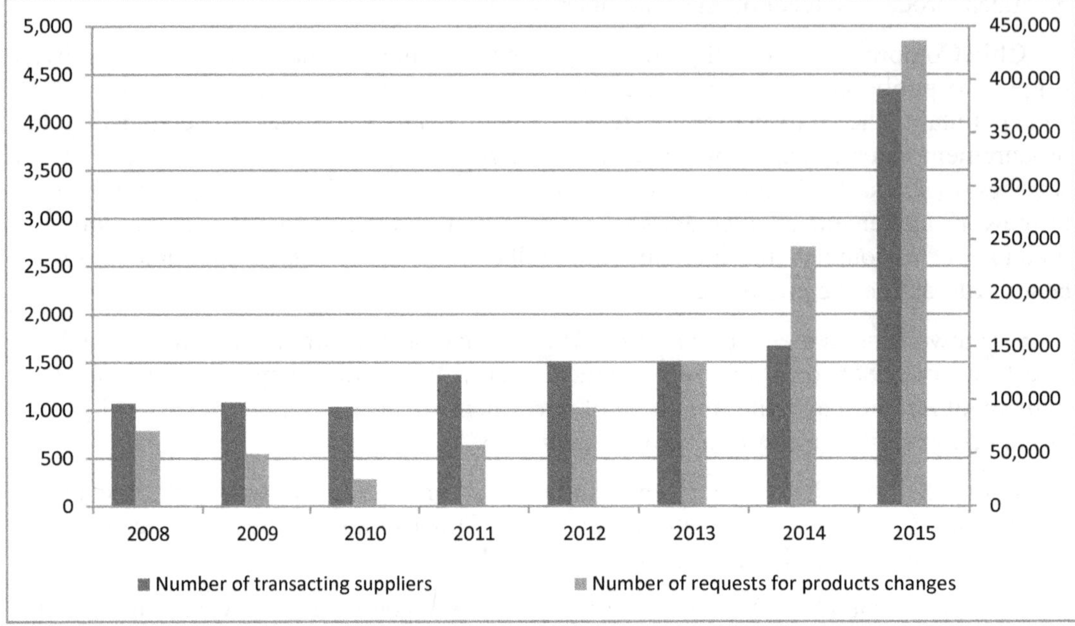

Source: Information provided by ChileCompra.

The architecture, functioning and use of ChileCompra Express over time show the success of ChileCompra in using framework agreements to achieve the overarching policy objectives of inclusiveness and openness of the public procurement system to Chilean suppliers of all size. Between 2010 and 2015, the number of transacting suppliers increased by almost 180% (Figure 1.3). It represents the largest virtual store in the country and is almost equivalent to the entire private electronic commerce in Chile.[3]

However, there are inherent operational and conceptual challenges alongside these successes, which hinder the overall efficiency of the system. Incremental evolution of the system could enhance its efficiency, its manageability and the overall benefits that framework agreements could bring (aggregation of demands, rationalisation of purchases and pool of suppliers, standardisation of offerings, etc.).

Revisiting the design of framework agreements offers a great opportunity for ChileCompra to further strengthen the strategic approach of its centralised procurement function. These efforts would support the more general shift towards strategic procurement experienced in many OECD countries.

Figure 1.4. Approaches to procurement

Traditional approach to procurement

Value add
Level of effort
Stage in process
Initiate project
Identify needs & analyse the market
Specify requirements
Plan approach to market & evaluation
Approach market & select supplier
Negotiate & award contract
Manage contract & relationship
Review

Vs.

Strategic approach to procurement

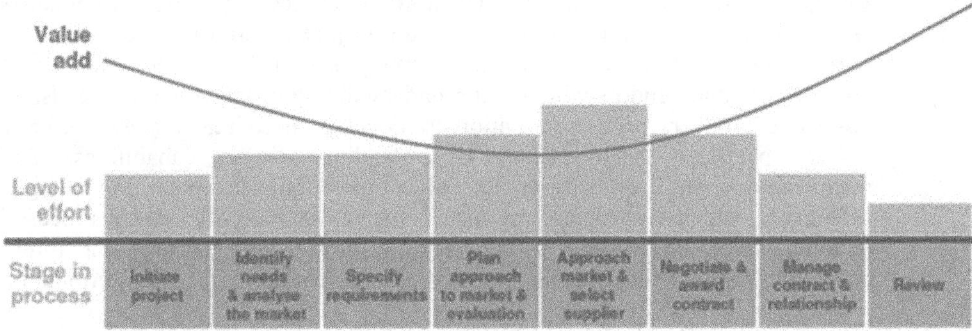

Source: Ministry of Business, Innovation and Employment of New Zealand (2011), *Mastering procurement a structured approach to strategic procurement*, www.procurement.govt.nz/procurement/for-agencies/strategic-procurement/mastering-procurement-the-guide.

Considering the current use of this procurement instrument, and its success in terms of inclusiveness, sound implementation of recommendations towards a more efficient system would require a cautious and phased approach to avoid drastic changes.

In order to better understand the different policy options available in the implementation and management of framework agreements, the OECD designed a survey (hereinafter the "Survey") focusing on the implementation of framework agreements by central purchasing bodies. This report includes analysis of the responses[4] received from the OECD and non-OECD countries that provided sound information on their experiences with this tool. The survey results are used to benchmark the practice of ChileCompra on centralised framework agreements against these countries.

Box 1.1. Principles of the OECD Recommendation linked to framework agreements

While the 2015 OECD Recommendation on Public Procurement spells out principles that are applicable to the entire public procurement cycle and to all procurement tools used by OECD member countries, some principles convey concepts that are closely linked to the centralised implementation and management of collaborative procurement instruments, such as framework agreements. The OECD Council notably:

1. **RECOMMENDS** that Adherents foster transparent and effective stakeholder **participation.**

To this end, Adherents should:

1. **Develop and follow a standard process when formulating changes to the public procurement system**. Such standard process should promote public consultations, invite the comments of the private sector and civil society, ensure the publication of the results of the consultation phase and explain the options chosen, all in a transparent manner.

2. **Engage in transparent and regular dialogues with suppliers and business associations to present public procurement objectives and to assure a correct understanding of markets.** Effective communication should be conducted to provide potential vendors with a better understanding of the country's needs, and government buyers with information to develop more realistic and effective tender specifications by better understanding market capabilities. Such interactions should be subject to due fairness, transparency and integrity safeguards, which vary depending on whether an active procurement process is ongoing. Such interactions should also be adapted to ensure that foreign companies participating in tenders receive transparent and effective information.

3. **Provide opportunities for direct involvement of relevant external stakeholders** in the procurement system with a view to increase transparency and integrity while assuring an adequate level of scrutiny, provided that confidentiality, equal treatment and other legal obligations in the procurement process are maintained.

2. **RECOMMENDS** that Adherents develop processes to drive **Efficiency** throughout the public procurement cycle in satisfying the needs of the government and its citizens.

To this end, Adherents should:

1. **Streamline the public procurement system and its institutional frameworks.** Adherents should evaluate existing processes and institutions to identify functional overlap, inefficient silos and other causes of waste. Where possible, a more service-oriented public procurement system should then be built around efficient and effective procurement processes and workflows to reduce administrative red tape and costs, for example through shared services.
2. **Implement sound technical processes to satisfy customer needs efficiently.** Adherents should take steps to ensure that procurement outcomes meet the needs of customers, for instance by developing appropriate technical specifications, identifying appropriate award criteria, ensuring adequate technical expertise among proposal evaluators, and ensuring adequate resources and expertise are available for contract management following the award of a contract.

Box 1.1. Principles of the OECD Recommendation linked to framework agreements *(continued)*

3. **Develop and use tools to improve procurement procedures, reduce duplication and achieve greater value for money**, including centralised purchasing, framework agreements, e-catalogues, dynamic purchasing, e-auctions, joint procurements and contracts with options. Application of such tools across sub-national levels of government, where appropriate and feasible, could further drive efficiency.

3. **RECOMMENDS** that Adherents develop a procurement workforce with the Capacity to continually deliver value for money efficiently and effectively.

To this end, Adherents should:

1. **Ensure that procurement officials meet high professional standards for knowledge, practical implementation and integrity by providing a dedicated and regularly updated set of tools**, for example, sufficient staff in terms of numbers and skills, recognition of public procurement as a specific profession, certification and regular trainings, integrity standards for public procurement officials and the existence of a unit or team analysing public procurement information and monitoring the performance of the public procurement system.

2. **Provide attractive, competitive and merit-based career options for procurement officials**, through the provision of clear means of advancement, protection from political interference in the procurement process and the promotion of national and international good practices in career development to enhance the performance of the procurement workforce.

3. **Promote collaborative approaches with knowledge centres such as universities, think tanks or policy centres to improve skills and competences of the procurement workforce**. The expertise and pedagogical experience of knowledge centres should be enlisted as a valuable means of expanding procurement knowledge and upholding a two-way channel between theory and practice, capable of boosting application of innovation to public procurement systems.

4. **RECOMMENDS** that Adherents drive performance improvements through **Evaluation** of the effectiveness of the public procurement system from individual procurements to the system as a whole, at all levels of government where feasible and appropriate.

To this end, Adherents should:

1. **Assess periodically and consistently the results of the procurement process.** Public procurement systems should collect consistent, up-to-date and reliable information and use data on prior procurements, particularly regarding price and overall costs, in structuring new needs assessments, as they provide a valuable source of insight and could guide future procurement decisions.

2. **Develop indicators to measure performance, effectiveness and savings of the public procurement system** for benchmarking and to support strategic policy making on public procurement.

Source: OECD (2015b), *Recommendation of the Council on Public Procurement*, OECD, Paris, www.oecd.org/gov/ethics/OECD-Recommendation-on-Public-Procurement.pdf.

Pursuing common objectives: The multiple forms of framework agreements

Framework agreements across countries have different structures, implement different mechanisms and sometimes use different names. A framework agreement may be defined by a processual explanation, which says that a framework agreement is commonly understood as a contractual instrument with one or more economic operators for the supply of goods, services and, in some cases, works. The purpose of the framework agreement is to establish under which terms governing contracts are awarded by one or more contracting authorities (CAs), under its principles and requirements.

Centralised framework agreements are implemented by a central purchasing body (CPB) on behalf of CAs. The tripartite relationship implied by this type of instrument (CPB – CAs – Suppliers), and the benefits provided by framework agreements, depend on the nature of the links between these different entities.

The level of commitment from the demand and the supply sides to the use of framework agreements will affect its functioning as it provides an indication of the likelihood of effective trade activities between the parties. Considering their inherent revenue uncertainty, the effectiveness of framework agreements for both sides will depend on this commitment.

When demand side commitment is weak, and contracting authorities are not required to purchase available products through a framework agreement, the attractiveness of this instrument to suppliers may be limited. When the supply side commitment is weak, and does not entail mandatory acceptance of orders, efficiencies for the contracting authorities may be questioned. The primary role of CPBs regarding framework agreements is, therefore, to try to reconcile their flexibility with reasonable visibility on likely procurement activities.

The overall structure of framework agreements could help to transform the role of the central purchasing body from an intermediary to an enabler.

Figure 1.5. The role of CPBs

1. Two opposite sides of the bridge

2. An evolving relationship with both sides changing the CPB's role

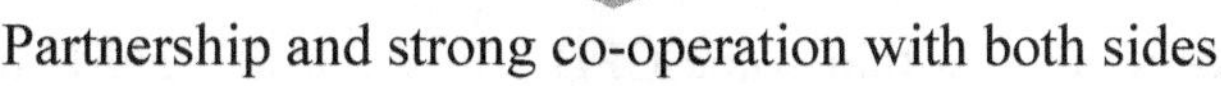

3. Two partners …. and an enabler

Source: OECD (2014), *Manual on Framework Agreements*, OECD, Paris.

This tripartite relationship surrounding the management and use of framework agreements could also have financial consequences. In several countries, CPBs generate budget resources from the use of framework agreements. At the same time, the Survey showed that the practice of CPBs receiving fees by suppliers or by contracting authorities is divided among countries (Figure 1.6).

Figure 1.6. Fees paid to CPBs for the use of framework agreements

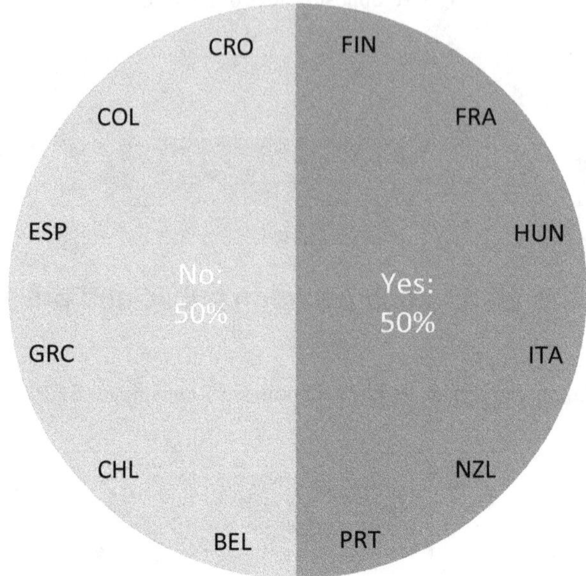

Source: OECD (2015c), *Survey on Centralised Framework Agreements*, OECD, Paris.

Previous surveys suggest that some CPBs[5] in the European Union receive some fees from suppliers (OECD, 2011b), which usually amount to between 0.6% and 2% of the invoiced turnover generated under the framework agreement. Such a system could provide CPBs with incentives to develop and implement performing framework agreements, since a share of their revenue directly derives from their use.

However, this system could also drive up prices under framework agreements, since the revenues, or a share of them, will depend on amounts invoiced. This potential effect would be mitigated in Chile, as the law authorises contracting authorities to purchase outside the framework agreements if terms and financial conditions are found to be more favourable.

The processual definition just explored only partially describes what framework agreements are and how they are understood and used by countries. Another way of defining framework agreements is to look at their purpose as a strategic procurement tool where processing costs, both at the implementation and administration levels are, or should be, outweighed by the benefits provided in terms of simplification, rationalisation or participation.

This second way of defining framework agreements provides for an additional decisive factor on the structure and functioning of framework agreements: they are not suited for all procurement activities. Whether decisions are made on the basis of shares of procurement expenditures, recurrence of purchases or nature of the markets, implementing framework agreements requires informed decisions that are often based on transactional information.

While the quality and reliability of transactional information is paramount to support any general move towards strategic procurement, this is even more acute for the strategic implementation and management of framework agreements. In 2014, more than 800 000 purchase orders were issued by Chilean contracting authorities under framework agreements. However, almost 15% of these orders were not correctly identified in the system, which means that ChileCompra cannot retrieve sufficient information on 8.75%, in terms of value, of public expenditure channelled through framework agreements, which amounts to USD 164 million.

Notes

1 Article 30 of Law 19 886 on Public Procurement (Ley de Bases Sobre Contratos Administrivos de Suministro y Prestacion de Servicios).

2 Regulation of Law 19 886 (Reglamento de la Ley n°19.886 de Bases Sobre Contratos Administrivos de Suministro y Prestacion de Servicios).

3 According to the Santiago Chamber of Commerce estimates, the e-commerce in Chile during 2014 amounted to USD 2 billion.

4 The survey was sent to Austria, Belgium, Canada, Chile, Colombia, Costa Rica, Croatia, Denmark, Estonia, Finland, France, Greece, Hungary, Iceland, Ireland, Italy, Korea, New Zealand, Portugal, Slovenia, Spain, Sweden, Switzerland, the United Kingdom and the United States. Responses were received from 11 OECD countries - namely, Belgium, Canada, Chile, Finland, France, Greece, Hungary, Italy, New Zealand, Portugal and Spain - and 2 non-OECD countries, Colombia and Costa Rica.

5 Hansel in Finland, SKI in Denmark, Buying Solutions in the United Kingdom and the Swedish CPBs.

References

EC (2011), *Evaluation Report: Impact and Effectiveness of EU Public Procurement Legislation – Part 1*, Commission Staff Working Paper, SEC (2011) 853 final, European Commission, Brussels, http://ec.europa.eu/internal_market/publicprocurement/docs/modernising_rules/er853_1_en.pdf (accessed 27 January 2016).

Ministry of Business, Innovation and Employment of New Zealand (2011), *Mastering procurement, a structured approach to strategic procurement*, www.procurement.govt.nz/procurement/for-agencies/strategic-procurement/mastering-procurement-the-guide.

OECD (2015a), *Government at a Glance 2015*, OECD Publishing, Paris, http://dx.doi.org/10.1787/gov_glance-2015-en.

OECD (2015b), *Recommendation of the Council on Public Procurement*, OECD, Paris, http://www.oecd.org/gov/ethics/OECD-Recommendation-on-Public-Procurement.pdf.

OECD (2015c), *Survey on Centralised Framework Agreements*, OECD, Paris.

OECD (2014), *Manual on Framework Agreements*, OECD, Paris.

OECD (2012), *OECD 2012 Survey on Public Procurement*, OECD, Paris.

OECD (2011a), *Government at a Glance 2011*, OECD Publishing, Paris, http://dx.doi.org/10.1787/gov_glance-2011-en.

OECD (2011b), *Centralised Purchasing Systems in the European Union*, SIGMA Papers, No. 47, OECD Publishing, Paris, http://dx.doi.org/10.1787/5kgkgqv703xw-en.

Chapter 2.

Strategies for implementing collaborative procurement instruments in Chile

Deciding to implement collaborative procurement instruments, such as framework agreements, requires detailed analyses of both the demand and the supply side to ensure that these instruments meet their underlying objectives. This chapter analyses concepts such as demand heterogeneity and supply uncertainty, which are central to the cost-benefit analysis of the implementation of procurement tools. It also highlights common practices across countries in the definition of procurement strategies.

A framework agreement is a legal procurement instrument that can help to rationalise and aggregate procurement needs, hence increasing public sector purchasing power. The OECD Recommendation on Public Procurement (OECD, 2015a) calls upon countries to develop processes that drive efficiency throughout the public procurement cycle. The Recommendation notably indicates that countries should: "develop and use tools to improve procurement procedures, reduce duplication and achieve greater value for money, including centralised purchasing, framework agreements, e-catalogues, dynamic purchasing, e-auctions, joint procurement and contract with options."

Framework agreements are part of many countries' procurement toolbox, along with other options that aim to increase the overall efficiency of public procurement systems. They can be beneficial to suppliers and provide them with longer, more stable and visible contractual relationships with public entities. However, because of their nature, framework agreements should be carefully implemented, as they do not contain contractual commitments towards the ordering of goods or services.

Demand heterogeneity and supply uncertainty require specific procurement strategies

As in many OECD countries, framework agreements in Chile are set up by the centralised purchasing body (CPB) on behalf of contracting authorities, which can be portrayed as the final users.

Figure 2.1. CPBs in charge of managing framework agreements

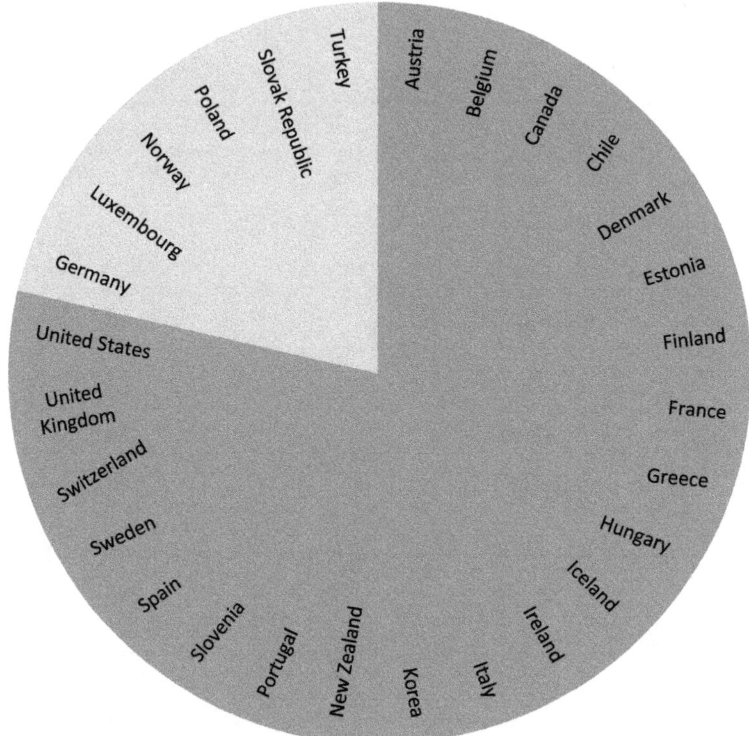

Source: Adapted from OECD (2015b), *Government at a Glance 2015*, OECD Publishing, Paris. http://dx.doi.org/10.1787/gov_glance-2015-en.

Although this system allows the CPB to have greater control of the definition of the corresponding procurement strategies, there are inherent challenges in ensuring that such a centralised procurement instrument meets decentralised needs.

Procurement strategies adapted to framework agreements should respond to different and sometimes contradictory objectives. Governments have increased their use of framework agreements to achieve costs savings and generate productivity gains (OECD, 2013a). Framework agreements can generate operational and administrative efficiencies by reducing red tape costs and delivering economies of scale, however, they also need to address the likely heterogeneity of needs across contracting authorities, and the possible different regulatory frameworks in which they are operating.

Highly disposable and standardised products will create an appetite for defining procurement strategies aimed at reducing costs. More complex or critical goods or services could lead to strategies that minimise the likelihood of the disruption of supply or that promote quality over prices. As such, it is key to adapt procurement strategies to the specificities of the goods or services to be procured.

Achieving the overarching objectives of framework agreements requires that analysis is undertaken of the demand, procurement needs and patterns of the purchasing entities (Nollet and Beaulieu, 2005). Information sources will greatly depend on whether a new framework agreement should be implemented, or if demand analysis concerns the renewal of an existing instrument.

Demand analysis should provide information on historical procurement trends in specific product categories and possible associated services; however, it also needs to closely look at the structure and characteristics of the demand side in terms of budget flexibility and mandatory recourse to framework agreements. Where framework agreements are used voluntarily, the corresponding potential budget should be cautiously assessed as it further reinforces revenue uncertainty.

An assessment of the market capabilities to respond to the CPB's request to implement a framework agreement is also essential during its preparation. Implementing efficient procurement strategies for the award of framework agreements involves understanding market performance and concentration (Church and Ware, 2000), as well as gathering information about the price structure of the targeted goods or services. The role of the price structures is more pronounced when considering that economies of scale can only occur when suppliers are able to operate at a lower unit cost, i.e. when production costs comprise a noticeable fraction of fixed costs, independent of production scales (Albano, 2010). Colombia has recognised the essential role of market studies in preparing a framework agreement and has established the minimum acceptable content for market studies (Box 2.1).

Box 2.1. Minimum acceptable content for market studies in Colombia

Colombian procurement statutes require government purchasing groups to undertake a "preliminary study" before they commence a procurement process. In the past, such studies have largely dealt with the nature of the procurement and procurement process, and the intended contractual terms and conditions, and so were not true market studies. Article 15 of the Decree 1510 of 2013 now specifically requires Colombian government officials to undertake a market analysis before a procurement process is commenced. Despite these legislative changes, few public procurement officials in Colombia prepare market studies and or have the skills to carry out such a study. To address this issue, *Colombia Compra Efficiente* established the minimum acceptable content for market studies through a manual published in 2013 and updated in 2014, which can be used by Colombian procurement agencies when they undertake their market studies (CCE, 2014).

Market studies should identify the characteristics and specifications of the:

- goods and services to be purchased
- existing and potential suppliers
- alternative products
- price trends over time
- differences in prices between private and public procurement markets
- costs and other competitive variables.

Market studies should be conducted by individuals with procurement and/or research expertise, who are provided with sufficient time and resources. The development of a training strategy and the implementation of a training action could provide procurement staff with the necessary expertise to conduct effective market studies.

Sources:

CCE (2014), "Guia para la elaboracion de estudios de sector", Colombia Compra Eficiente, https://www.colombiacompra.gov.co/sites/default/files/manuales/cce_guia_estudio_sector_web.pdf.

Adapted from OECD (2016), Towards Efficient Public Procurement in Colombia: Making the Difference, OECD Public Governance Reviews, OECD Publishing, Paris. http://dx.doi.org/10.1787/9789264252103-en.

On the basis of these preliminary analyses, tailored procurement strategies adapted to framework agreements would contribute to defining the design of the tender documentation. They would also try to reconcile the inherent uncertainty (suppliers are not promised to receive any revenue out of framework agreements) of such an instrument, with the reasonable certainty setting the ground for competitive proposals (suppliers are not incentivised to propose attractive terms and conditions if contextual information is not sufficient).

Stakeholders' participation (contracting authorities, suppliers, audit agencies) in the definition of the tender structure could also help foster inclusive framework agreements that would yield benefits and additional efficiency gains (greater coverage, better co-ordination and feedback).

Figure 2.2. Assessment of demand and supply sides

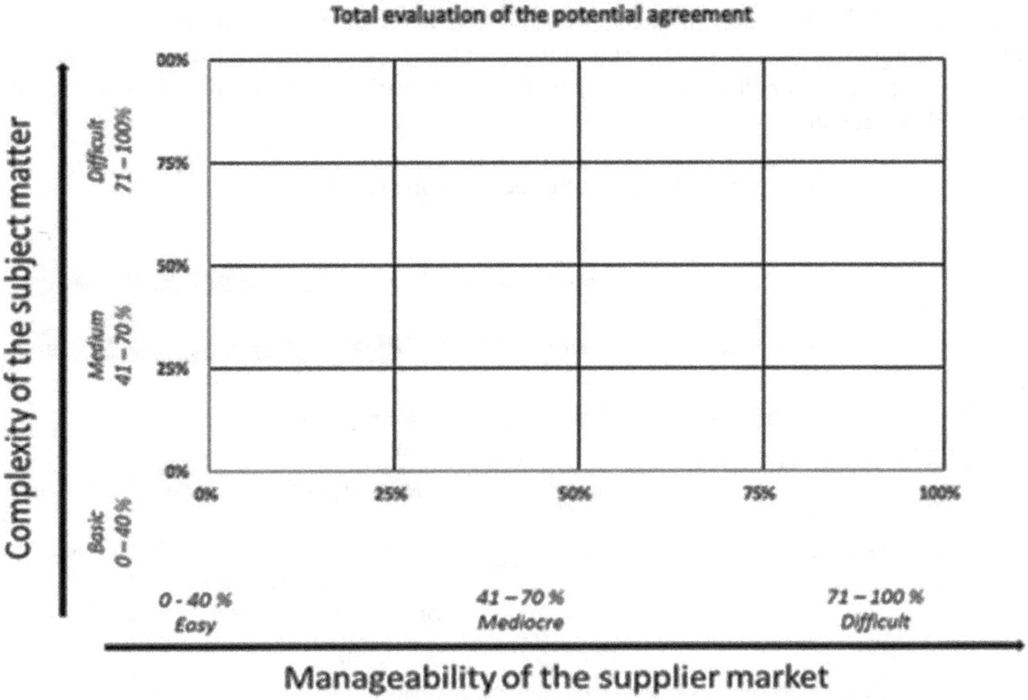

Source: OECD (2014), *Manual on Framework Agreements*, OECD, Paris.

Figure 2.2 illustrates, from a different perspective, major principles that allow an assessment of the feasibility of implementing framework agreements. CPBs need to obtain information on the amount of purchases and the number of orders, as well as estimating the complexity of the subject matter, both from the contracting authority (CA) perspective and in terms of the product characteristics. CPBs also need to evaluate the manageability of the supply side by assessing industry structure and market capabilities.

In line with the OECD Recommendation on Public Procurement, external stakeholders can be involved in the definition of the procurement strategy. One option is for procurement authorities to benefit from existing market studies previously carried out by competition authorities. For example, Peru's competition authorities have developed market studies in specific areas. Several market studies were conducted in the past five years, including on competition in public procurement at the regional level, the domestic market for commercial airlines, the health system, the notary service market, the mobile market and the distribution of natural gas (OECD, 2015c).

Implementing framework agreements is a strategic choice based on robust analysis

According to the OECD Survey, all countries devote efforts to the demand analysis stage before implementing or renewing a framework agreement. Considering the overall architecture of this procurement instrument, sources of information could be found in e-procurement systems and/or by conducting interviews or meetings with contracting authorities and/or suppliers.

Consulting contracting authorities is considered as best practice for all countries that responded to the Survey, however, it is mandatory only for 9% of respondents. In New Zealand and Italy, this consultation process follows a uniformed methodology for all framework agreements, or is reported into a standardised format. In Chile, a specific timetable for the consultation of contracting authorities is only developed for new framework agreements.

Figure 2.3. Data collected to define future needs

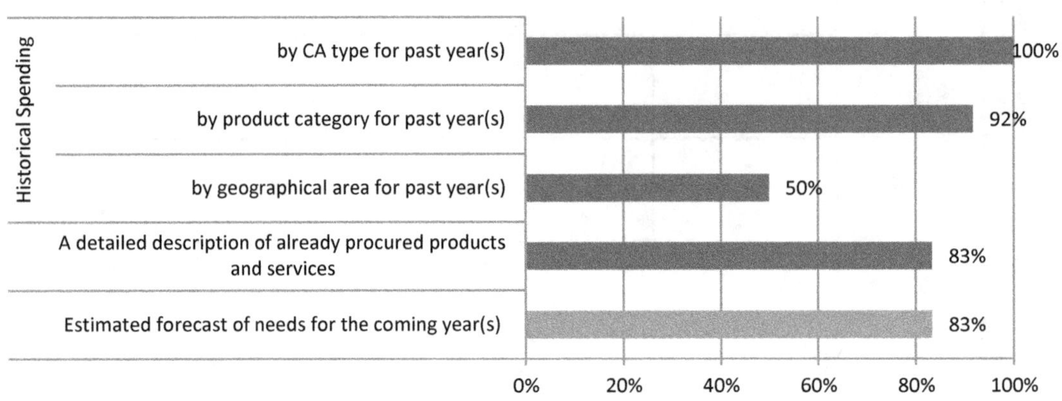

Note: Lighter blue colour indicates where Chile does not take part.

Source: OECD (2015), *Survey on Centralised Framework Agreements*, OECD Paris.

Past procurement information on electronic systems is also commonly used to determine future needs. This information is either collected through centralised e-procurement systems, such as in France, or with the assistance of external authorities that monitor public spending, like the anti-corruption authority in Italy (ANAC).

In parallel to estimating needs from a financial perspective, central purchasing bodies in the OECD countries surveyed are carrying out discussions and analyses to structure the demand of contracting authorities. Almost two thirds of the respondents indicated liaising with the most relevant contracting authorities to obtain detailed information about their procurement trends and patterns.

Although suppliers are frequently consulted, an analysis of their past performance is less frequently practiced in the demand analysis stage.

Figure 2.4. Measures implemented in the demand analysis stage

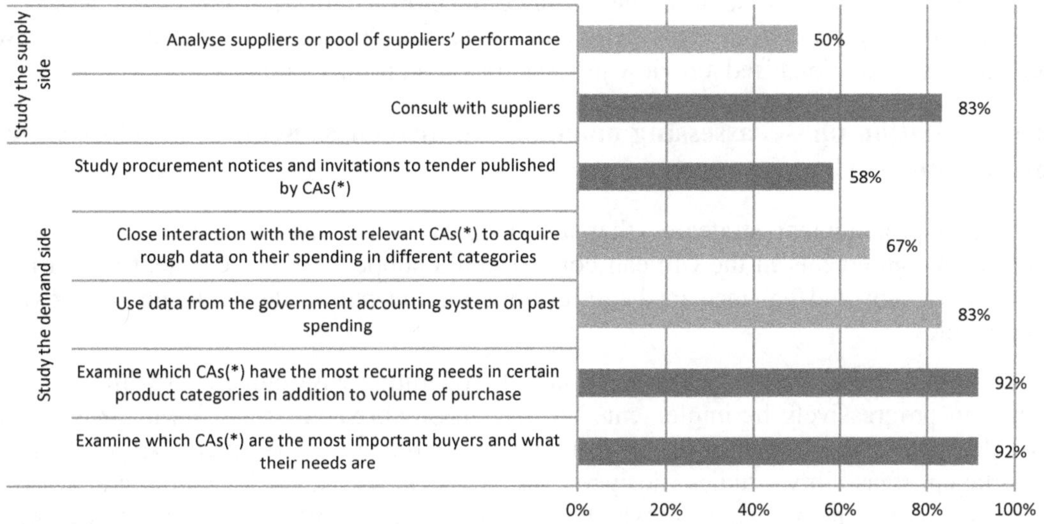

Study the supply side
Analyse suppliers or pool of suppliers' performance
50%
Consult with suppliers
83%
Study the demand side
Study procurement notices and invitations to tender published by CAs(*)
58%
Close interaction with the most relevant CAs(*) to acquire rough data on their spending in different categories
67%
Use data from the government accounting system on past spending
83%
Examine which CAs(*) have the most recurring needs in certain product categories in addition to volume of purchase
92%
Examine which CAs(*) are the most important buyers and what their needs are
92%
0%
20%
40%
60%
80%
100%

Note: Lighter blue colour indicates where Chile does not take part. (*) CA means contracting authorities.

Source: OECD (2015) Survey on Centralised Framework Agreements, OECD Paris

Over 50% of respondents to the OECD survey undertake a cost-benefit analysis to identify whether or not a framework agreement is the most efficient procurement route. Based on country experiences, this feasibility study encompasses analyses of both demand and supply sides structures and patterns, the existence of product alternatives, or the level of competitiveness of the market.

Figure 2.5. Development of feasibility study for each framework agreement

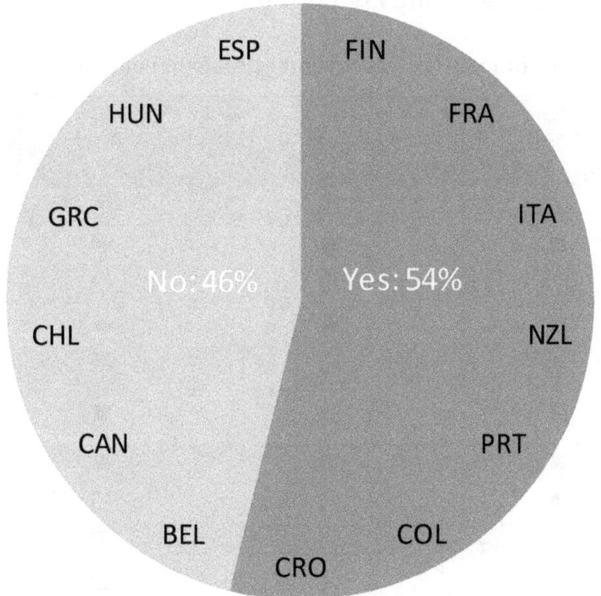

ESP
FIN
HUN
FRA
GRC
ITA
No: 46%
Yes: 54%
CHL
NZL
CAN
PRT
BEL
COL
CRO

Source: OECD (2015) Survey on Centralised Framework Agreements, OECD Paris

While most of the respondents implement feasibility studies depending on the nature of the goods or services, some countries have developed more formalised process. For example, Finland has developed a template for feasibility studies (see Annex B). New Zealand has institutionalised a review process for each product category.

In the pre-solicitation phase, assessing market responsiveness helps to maximise the efficiency of framework agreements

Sound procurement strategies that are adapted to the nature and specificities of framework agreements in the Chilean context could support a more efficient use of this legal instrument and enhance its benefits both for the public demand and the private supply sides.

In light of OECD country practices, and the operating environment in Chile, further steps can progressively be implemented to design procurement strategies that allow for the effective and efficient use of framework agreements. However, before this is undertaken, feasibility studies designed in accordance with ChileCompra's overall objectives could help to decide whether or not a framework agreement is the most suitable procurement tool to respond to public demand.

ChileCompra could develop structured feasibility studies to guide its decision to implement framework agreements

In accordance with Article 30 d) of the Law on Public Procurement, framework agreements are implemented either based on the discretionary decision of the ChileCompra or following the request of one or more contracting authorities. However, Article 14 of the Bylaws on Public Procurement further details that implementation of framework agreements is always subject to an opportunity assessment carried out by ChileCompra. The latter has discretionary powers on deciding the appropriateness to implement such a procurement instrument. Various procurement instruments sitting alongside framework agreements are used by OECD countries.

Figure 2.6. Use of innovative procurement tools in central government (2012)

	Framework agreement	Contracts with options	Prequalification systems	Electronic reverse auctioning
Australia	☒	☒	☒	☒
Austria	■	■	☒	☐
Belgium	☐	☐	☐	☐
Canada	■	■	■	☐
Chile	■	☐	☒	☐
Czech Republic	■	☒	■	☒
Denmark	■	■	■	☒
Estonia	■	☐	☐	☐
Finland	☒	☒	☒	☒
France	☒	☒	☐	☐
Germany	■	■	☒	☐
Hungary	☒	☒	☒	☒

Figure 2.6. Use of innovative procurement tools in central government (2012) *(continued)*

	Framework agreement	Contracts with options	Prequalification systems	Electronic reverse auctioning
Iceland	■	☒	☒	□
Ireland	■	□	□	□
Israel	■	■	☒	■
Italy	■	■	☒	□
Japan	□	☒	■	☒
Korea	☒	☒	■	□
Luxembourg	☒	□	□	□
Mexico	■	□	□	●
Netherlands	■	■	□	□
New Zealand	☒	☒	☒	□
Norway	■	■	☒	□
Poland	☒	☒	□	☒
Portugal	■	□	■	☒
Slovak Republic	■	☒	☒	■
Slovenia	■	⑥	⑤	❄
Spain	■	❄	❄	□
Sweden	☒	☒	☒	□
Switzerland	■	■	■	□
Turkey	■	□	■	□
United Kingdom	■	☒	☒	☒
United States	■	■	■	☒

Total OECD

	Framework agreement	Contracts with options	Prequalification systems	Electronic reverse auctioning
■	22	10	10	3
☒	9	14	15	11
□	2	9	8	19

■ Tool is routinely used in all procuring entities

☒ Tool is routinely used in some procuring entities

□ Tool is not routinely used

Source: OECD (2013b), "Innovative tools in public procurement", in *Government at a Glance 2013*, OECD Publishing, Paris, http://dx.doi.org/10.1787/gov_glance-2013-45-en.

Deciding upon the implementation of framework agreements is subject to a cost-benefit analysis. The cost assessment heavily relies on the CPB's understanding and accurate estimate of the administrative tasks required to prepare, award and manage this instrument. Product categories with a large pool of suppliers, and that are prone to regular product updates or modifications, will directly increase the overall cost of this procurement instrument.

While cost assessments follow a somewhat identical methodology, the benefits of a framework agreement could be multidimensional, depending on the overall objectives of the CPB towards its creation. If the main objectives relate to the inclusiveness of the system, i.e. providing business opportunities for as many suppliers as possible, benefits would likely comprise an assessment of the concentration of the market in the specific product category. Activities should also include an analysis of past procurement expenditure that focuses on the number of contracting authorities that have purchased corresponding goods or services.

Should the objectives be to increase the efficiency of public spending and generate economies of scale, the benefits are to be found on the potential of framework agreements to aggregate a large volume of procurement expenditure and to structure internal demand. In this respect, product homogeneity plays a central role regarding the ability of framework agreements to effectively aggregate demand. For those product categories where a large range of goods and/or services are available, the recourse to framework agreements is not likely to produce the expected effects on economies of scale. Benefits linked to the aggregation of demand could leverage purchasing power and contribute to broader policy objectives, such as the development of open government programmes. The absence of concerted, centralised procurement policies for the purchase of IT hardware could hinder this type of initiative, as has been evidenced in Finland.

ChileCompra could promote a regional structure for specific framework agreements to foster competition and ease access to procurement opportunities to small and medium-sized enterprises (SMEs)

Although call for tenders already allow bidders to select regions in which they propose to operate, ChileCompra could further embed regional aspects into tender documentation, where deemed appropriate. Transforming an operational requirement into a structuring element of the tender could provide several benefits.

The regional distribution of orders under framework agreements could signal geographical heterogeneity in terms of the needs of contracting authorities in Chile (Figure 2.7). While the metropolitan area of Santiago (region XIII) generates almost half of the orders in terms of number, which reflects the concentration of contracting authorities in the capital, Bio-Bio (region VIII), whose area is less than 25% of the Magallanes area (region XII), orders three times more products under this framework agreement.

Figure 2.7. Regional distribution of purchase orders (POs) under the framework agreement for vehicle accessories, tyres, and associated services

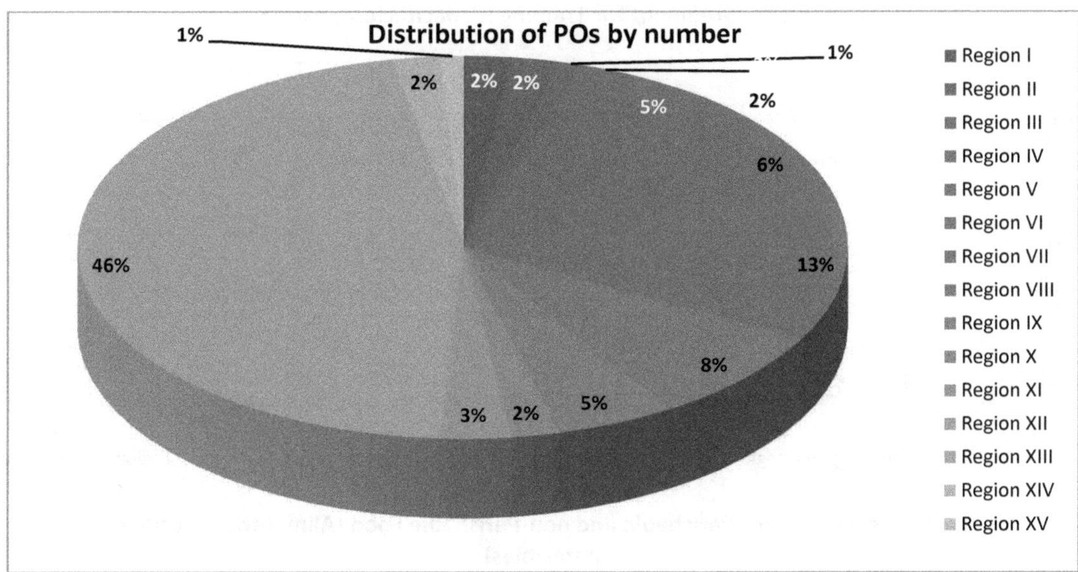

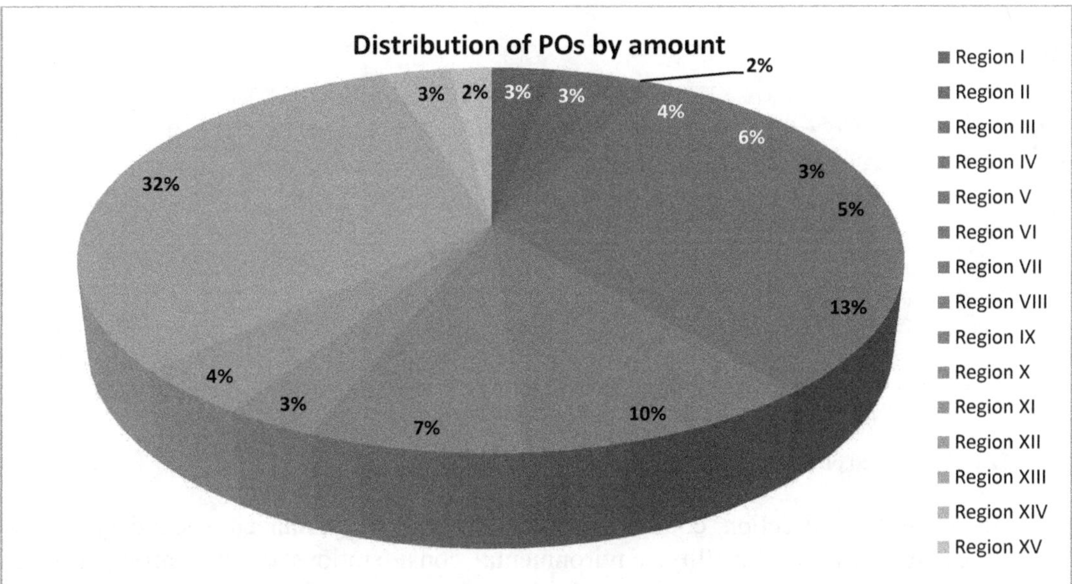

Source: OECD Analysis based on information provided by ChileCompra (2012-2015).

When looking at supplier distribution, only 22% of suppliers operate in all 15 regions, and most operate in only a few regions. Furthermore, almost 40% of suppliers operate in only 1 region (Figure 2.8), and this trend can be observed both for goods and services. Supported by more detailed analyses on suppliers' distribution, these elements could provide insights into the market structure, and the need for contracting authorities to allow for a tailored regional structure of tenders.

Figure 2.8. Regions in which suppliers operate (2015)

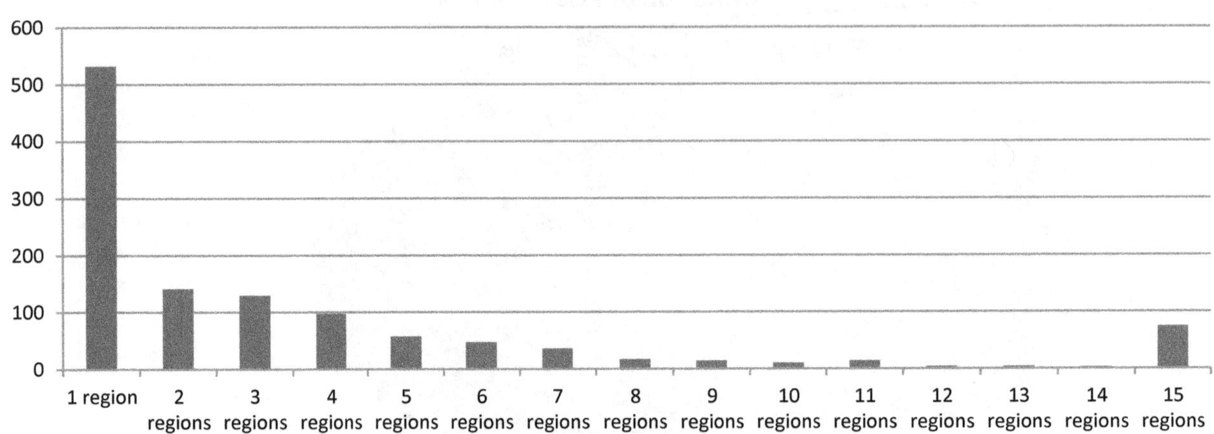

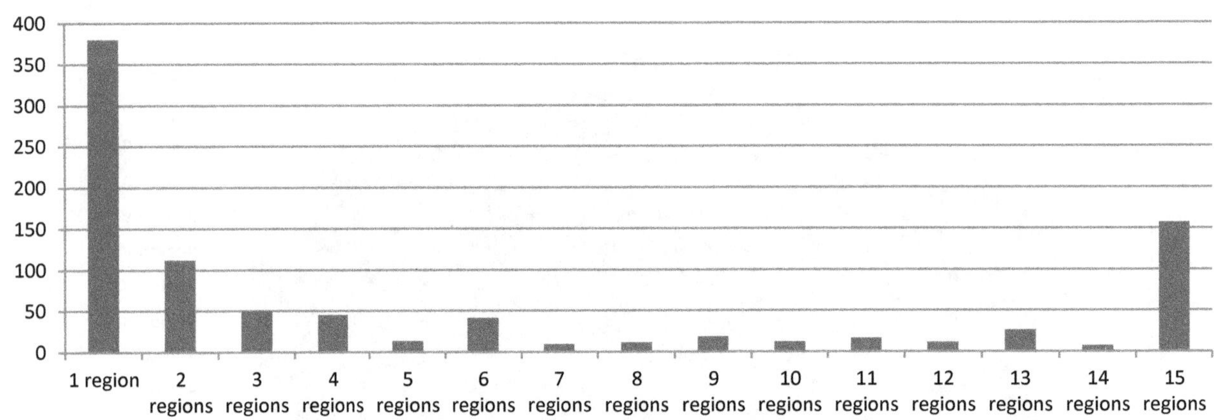

Source: OECD analysis based on information provided by Chilecompra.

Efforts in this direction could also help to integrate balanced secondary policy objectives, such as sustainability, environmental considerations or the participation of SMEs in procurement processes that lead to the award of framework agreements. However, thorough market analysis would be essential to support the potential benefits.

By disaggregating procurement needs into regional lots, ChileCompra could foster the participation of SMEs in the corresponding competitive procurement process, in which they may otherwise not have been able or interested to participate For example, deciding to structure the tender documentation relating to the provision of raw food in regional lots implies a procurement strategy that is directed to local producers rather than distributors. Provided that the market structure and business trends support this decision, it would further promote access by SMEs to public procurement opportunities, and also introduce environmental considerations.

However, these efforts should take due consideration of potential bid rigging or collusive tendering. Bid rigging occurs when "businesses, that would otherwise be expected to compete, secretly conspire to raise prices or lower the quality of goods or services for purchasers who wish to acquire products or services through a bidding process" (OECD, 2012). Dividing tenders into administrative regional lots could favour market allocation whereby bidders secretly agree not to compete in certain geographic areas.

The OECD Recommendation on Fighting Bid Rigging in Public Procurement provides guidance to procurement officials on designing public tenders to reduce bid rigging (design checklist). They notably suggest reducing predictability in tender design. Therefore, a division into geographic areas that does not follow the administrative division of the country, but rather, when appropriate, regional divisions of the market according to geographical allocation of demand and supply, could help minimise the occurrence of such behaviour.

Chilecompra could consider adapting the duration of framework agreements in accordance with complexity and market trends

Most of the existing framework agreements implemented by ChileCompra last six years, which is relatively high, according to the recent benchmarking exercise. In the European Union, the maximum duration of framework agreements is four years, save in exceptional circumstances. An initial duration could be two to three years, with the possibility of up to two prolongations of one year, depending on the performance, the achievement of objectives, or the need to update the instrument. During the term of this type of closed framework agreement, competition is locked and additional suppliers cannot enter into the agreement.

Defining the duration of a framework agreement continues the trade-off initiated when assessing the need to create a framework agreement, as the time and resources required for its implementation and the benefits that it may yield must be considered. On the one hand, a short duration would provide regular market updates and allow central purchasing bodies to be constantly abreast of market developments and trends. However, this may limit the attractiveness for suppliers and expand processing costs for the central purchasing body. On the other hand, a longer duration could foster the development of stable contractual relationships, which may provide greater potential revenue for suppliers and increasing public purchasing power. However, a long duration might generate outdated offerings, which would be less attractive to end users or entail unnecessary additional product updates.

Carefully balancing decisions regarding the duration of framework agreements based on the nature of the product category (fast obsolescence, initial investment required, entry of new suppliers) and the structure of the corresponding market (competitiveness, openness) is therefore essential. ChileCompra could take these two criteria into account when assessing the optimal duration of its framework agreements.

In EU countries, a slightly different practice has been developed that enables suppliers to join existing collaborative procurement instruments, provided that they respond to minimum requirements. However, this procurement instrument, referred to as a dynamic purchasing system (or open framework agreements in some jurisdictions), is differentiated from a framework agreement in the European context. As opposed to framework agreements, dynamic purchasing systems only request suppliers to fulfil technical requirements at the initial competition stage. The second competition stage then provides for competition among suppliers on the financial aspects. Those two instruments are not exclusive and often provide complementary options to respond to collective government procurement.

On the basis of product and market characteristics, ChileCompra could consider implementing strategies aimed at differentiating instruments. This could further promote the participation of suppliers where fulfilling technical requirements is sufficient for identifying suitable suppliers. Entry points during the term of the agreement could be defined to allow additional suppliers to participate.

Strategic analysis could support choices relating to the aggregation and rationalisation of demand, which would increase ChileCompra's purchasing levers.

Framework agreements are commonly used as a strategic procurement tool to foster the aggregation and rationalisation of demand. By consolidating needs from end users, central purchasing bodies can leverage a global volume increase to obtain more competitive proposals from suppliers. This, however, requires more visibility on procurement spending.

Box 2.2. Aggregating demand in Australia

The Government of Western Australia developed eight smarter buying principles to help steer the public sector towards making better purchasing decisions, implementing better practice, and achieving value for money. These principles are illustrated by case studies relating to projects undertaken by one of the state agencies.

The Goldfields Esperance Regional Buying Centre initiated a group buying arrangement for airline travel within the Goldfields region. The establishment of the group buying arrangement has:

- Identified a contractor with fixed rates and conditions.
- Incorporated the needs of many agencies.
- Identified actual spend.
- Reduced time wasted when booking individual services.

Previous procurement process

Prior to the joint contract, there was no arrangement in place for air travel within the Goldfields region. As such, agencies were required to seek their own competitive quotes when the need arose. They operated in isolation and were not aware of what other agencies with the same needs had done previously, or what prices had been paid.

This process was time consuming and inefficient, and wasted considerable agency staff time that could be better utilised. Furthermore, because there was minimal understanding of the spend incurred by each agency, the potential for large volume buying could not be taken advantage of.

Changed procurement process

Discussions with members of the local client council identified that considerable time and money was spent by agencies chartering air services for travel in the Goldfields region. Little was known as to what the actual spend was, although estimates were around AUD 200 000 annually.

Box 2.2. Aggregating demand in Australia *(continued)*

There was recognition of the potential benefits of putting in place a group buying arrangement. This would enable all agencies in the region to access the one contract, enabling the buying to be undertaken more quickly and at a pre-determined price. The group buying arrangement was drafted incorporating two large users, the Departments of Education and Corrective Services (DoE), as well as other regional users. Aircraft requirements, regulations and local capabilities to deliver services were considered.

As part of an open tender process, the Regional Buying Centre sought offers from appropriately experienced, skilled and qualified aviation operators to provide ongoing management, operation and maintenance of aircraft charter services for state government agencies throughout the Goldfields region.

Improved outcomes

By aggregating air travel services and creating a single contract that could be used by all agencies requiring travel in the Goldfields region, the Regional Buying Centre has opened up communication between agencies that ordinarily operate in isolation.

"We discovered that lots of agencies required this service, and that many agencies were replicating the work already done by others," said Robert Tagliaferri, Senior Procurement Manager. "By talking to a few, we were able to nut out the general requirements and make a single contract that would address everyone's needs."

"Some of the conditions we've set encourage the agencies to talk more," said Robert. "For example, if DoE only has two people that need to go to a particular town, but a flight requires six passengers, it can contact some of the other agencies to see if they need to fly out too."

The new contract also means that if an agency has enough people to fill a flight, they can simply book the contracted supplier as opposed to chasing numerous quotes, which saves significant time and effort.

The group buying arrangement has also been successful in determining exactly how much money is being spent on regional air travel. "We originally thought the contract would be worth about AUD 600 000 over three years," said Robert. "But the more research and analysis we did, the higher the number climbed."

In fact, the original estimate has more than trebled to AUD 600 000 per yea,r and current spend analysis has indicated a contract value of $1.8 million over three years.

Benefits

By creating this contract as a joint arrangement, the Goldfields Esperance Regional Buying Centre has:

- Created a single contract with fixed prices.
- Reduced the level of duplicated procurement effort.
- Identified an area of significant government spend.
- Addressed the needs of many agencies.
- Encouraged a better working relationship between agencies.

Source: Government of Western Australia (2010), *Better Practice in Procurement, Case Studies*, Government Procurement, Department of Treasury and Finance, available at www.finance.wa.gov.au/cms/uploadedFiles/_Procurement/News/case_study_book.pdf?n=4582 (accessed 27 January 2016).

Governmental contracting authorities in Chile are obliged to use centralised framework agreements established by ChileCompra, in accordance with Article 30 d) of the Law on Public Procurement. While municipalities, army and police forces are not obliged to use centralised framework agreements, they can voluntarily adhere to them and benefit from the products and services offered.

One exception to the mandatory use of framework agreements by governmental entities lies with the identification of similar goods or services that have more competitive conditions outside of the framework agreements. This exception, along with the voluntary use by specific public entities, advocates for the most comprehensive possible consolidation of needs.

Figure 2.9. Coverage of the framework agreements (2014)

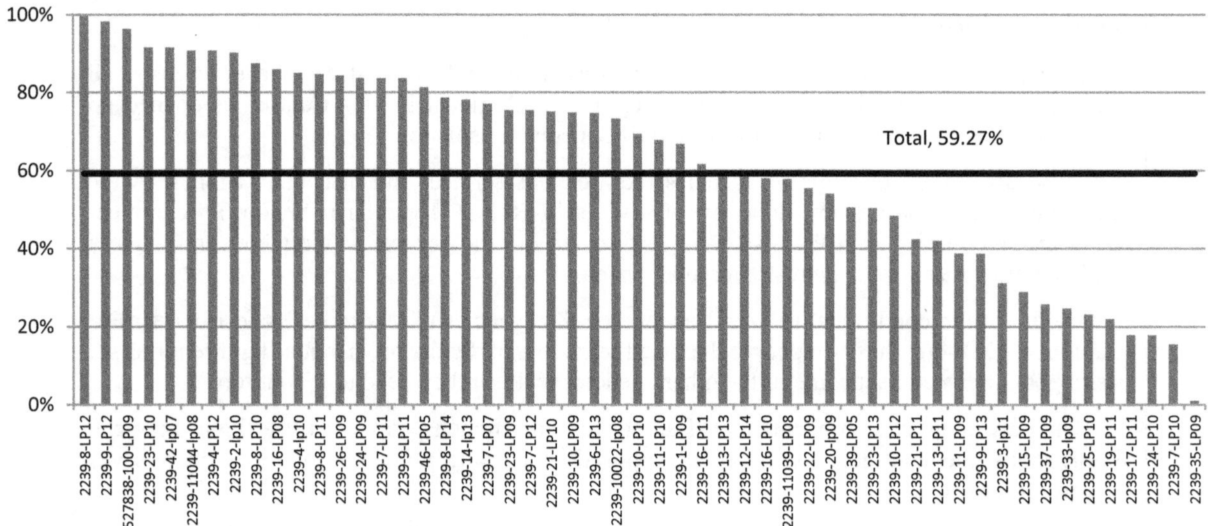

Note: Each bar represents framework agreements for different goods and services of ChileCompra

Source: OECD analysis based on information provided by ChileCompra.

On average, existing framework agreements in Chile covered around 59% of the corresponding public expenditure in 2014. Although reaching 100% of coverage of needs may be unrealistic, some product categories are lagging significantly behind the average, such as the framework agreement relating to data centre and associated services (17.85%) or training and education services (28.92%).

This issue poses two questions. The first relates to the assessment of the costs-benefits ratio, which is the basis on which decisions regarding the implementation of framework agreements are made. Framework agreements entail administrative costs deriving from implementation and management efforts. These costs should be outweighed by the benefits provided to the end users in terms of ease and speediness of procurement operations. A low level of coverage of public expenditure could signal dysfunctional framework agreements, which question the validity of the benefit assumption.

The second question concerns the process and amount of information relating to the needs of contracting authorities and market capacities. Global market analysis could provide ChileCompra with valuable insights into market concentration and major trends in specific sectors subject to the implementation of framework agreements. As part of this analysis, ChileCompra could further benefit from market studies carried out by the Chilean Competition Authority (*Fiscalía Nacional Económica*, FNE).

The sound design of framework agreement strategies heavily draws upon a thorough analysis of procurement spending and its patterns. Well-established processes at the demand analysis stage would provide ChileCompra with useful insights on end user behaviours and expectations, which would support the enhanced coverage of framework agreements.

The National Board of Student Aid and Scholarships (*Junta Nacional de Auxilio Escolar y Becas*, JUNAEB) comprises regional contracting authorities. It provides an example of a national institution that is structured into different regional contracting authorities, and illustrates the challenges and opportunities for the implementation of co-ordinated procurement decisions. As shown in Figure 2.10, procurement patterns differ substantially in terms of the number of purchase orders and the average amount of purchase orders. This information could fuel different analyses on procurement behaviours resulting in low value – high frequency purchase orders.

Figure 2.10. Contracting authorities' procurement patterns under framework agreements

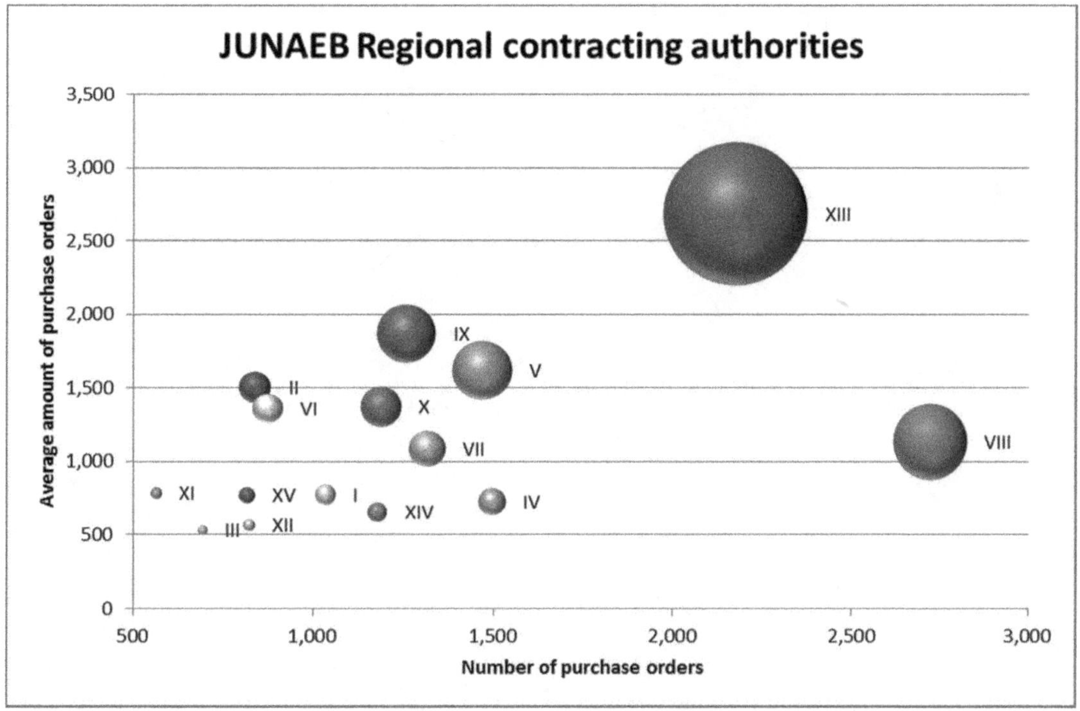

Note: The size of the circles represents the total volume of purchase orders, in terms of value.

Source: Analysis made by the OECD based on www.analiza.cl for purchase orders issued under framework agreements between 2008 and 2015.

By putting further emphasis on demand analysis, ChileCompra could strategically drive the use of framework agreements, which may result in a greater consolidation of purchases. However, these efforts would require the mobilisation of sufficient resources in number and skills. Considering the decentralisation of purchases under framework agreements, and the absence of integration of the platform managed by ChileCompra with the public finance management system, this work needs to be initiated sufficiently in advance of the procurement process.

For this reason, it may be desirable to test the impact of these efforts on the coverage of framework agreements and the overall efficiency of a pilot project. For example, framework agreements experiencing lower coverage of public expenditure could be subject to further demand analysis to adapt the procurement strategy. The outcomes of this analysis would help ChileCompra to address the weaknesses identified in the previous cycle.

References

Albano, G. L., A. Ballarin and M. Sparro (2010), "Framework Agreements and Repeated Purchases: the Basic Economics and a Case Study on the Acquisition of IT Services", *Journal of Public Procurement*, www.ippa.org/IPPC4/Proceedings/04EconomicsofProcurement/Paper4-1.pdf.

CCE (2014), "Guia para la 43laboración de estudios de sector", *Colombia Compra Eficiente*, https://www.colombiacompra.gov.co/sites/default/files/manuales/cce_guia_estudio_sector_web.pdf.

Church and Ware (2000), *Industrial Organisation, A strategic approach*, Mc Graw-Hill

Government of Western Australia (2010), *Better Practice in Procurement, Case Studies*, Government Procurement, Department of Treasury and Finance, available at www.finance.wa.gov.au/cms/uploadedFiles/_Procurement/News/case_study_book.pdf?n=4582 (accessed 27 January 2016).

Nollet and Beaulieu (2005), "Should an organisation join a purchasing group?", *Supply Chain Management*, Emerald Insight, http://dx.doi.org/10.1108/13598540510578333.

OECD (2016), *Towards Efficient Public Procurement in Colombia: Making the Difference*, OECD Public Governance Reviews, OECD Publishing, Paris, http://dx.doi.org/10.1787/9789264252103-en.

OECD (2015a), *Recommendation of the Council on Public Procurement*, OECD, Paris, http://www.oecd.org/gov/ethics/OECD-Recommendation-on-Public-Procurement.pdf.

OECD (2015b), *Government at a Glance 2015*, OECD Publishing, Paris. http://dx.doi.org/10.1787/gov_glance-2015-en.

OECD (2015c), *Competition and Market Studies in Latin America: The Case of Chile, Colombia, Costa Rica, Mexico, Panama and Peru*, OECD Publishing, Paris, http://www.oecd.org/daf/competition/competition-and-market-studies-in-latin-america2015.pdf.

OECD (2015d), *Survey on Centralised Framework Agreements*, OECD, Paris.

OECD (2014), *Manual on Framework Agreements*, OECD, Paris.

OECD (2013a), *Implementing the OECD Principles for Integrity in Public Procurement: Progress since 2008*, OECD Publishing, Paris, http://dx.doi.org/10.1787/9789264201385-en.

OECD (2013b), "Innovative tools in public procurement", in *Government at a Glance 2013*, OECD Publishing, Paris, http://dx.doi.org/10.1787/gov_glance-2013-45-en.

OECD (2012), *Recommendation of the OECD Council on Fighting Bid Rigging in Public Procurement*, OECD, Paris, www.oecd.org/daf/competition/RecommendationOnFightingBidRigging2012.pdf.

Chapter 3.

Enhancing competition to maximise the benefits of framework agreements

As value for money is the primary objective of public procurement, countries have to develop an environment that is conducive to competition by reducing the asymmetry of information between contracting authorities and economic operators, but also by raising awareness of procurement opportunities. This chapter analyses how ChileCompra could improve competition, and thus the efficiency of framework agreements when they are designed, by encouraging early engagement with suppliers, developing the capacity of the public procurement workforce, standardising goods and services, and reducing the number of awarded economic operators.

The creation of an environment conducive to competition is necessary to attract and retain the best suppliers

Public procurement involves the expenditure of large sums of public money, and given its magnitude, can impact the structure and functioning of competition in a market. The primary objective of an effective procurement policy is the promotion of efficiency and the achievement of the best "value for money."

Framework agreement is a widely-used procurement instrument to help address these objectives. Therefore, any contracting authority or central purchasing body (CPB) developing or managing framework agreements needs to create and ensure a competitive environment. A sound planning phase, grounded in thorough demand analysis, and sound market research and analysis will be key factors for the success of the framework agreement. Tender documents and specifications should, as a general rule, be clear, comprehensive, non-discriminatory, and have a focus on functional performance. The efficiency of the procurement process depends on the bidding model adopted and how the tender is designed, as well as on different mechanisms that favour a competitive environment, including the early engagement of suppliers and contracting authorities and the adequate standardisation of goods and services, which are further discussed in this chapter.

Compared to a contracting authority, a CPB running a framework agreement has more impact on the market, especially where the framework agreement is subject to mandatory use by the contracting authorities. To ensure that the framework agreement is designed and implemented in a sound manner, and that the needs of demand and supply sides are adequately met, suppliers and contracting authorities should be engaged in different stages of the tender.

There are two main reasons that could explain the benefits of engaging suppliers in different stages of the framework agreement:

1. Reduction of information asymmetry
2. Awareness of procurement opportunities

In the context of principal-agent problems, information asymmetry assumes that at least one party to a transaction has relevant information, whereas the other does not. The problem arises where the two parties have different interests and when the agent (a supplier) has more information than the principal (the CPB); meaning that the principal cannot directly ensure that the agent is always acting in the principal's best interests.

In procurement, it is acknowledged that suppliers have more information than the CPB on their costs, prices, market trends, products or services, and their substitutes. Therefore, meeting with a representative sample of suppliers could help decrease the information gap between the CPB and suppliers by collecting more credible and up-to-date information of the market. An example of this can be found in the framework agreement on cleaning services in Croatia (Box 3.1).

Box 3.1. A strategic sourcing and collaborative approach: Cleaning services in Croatia

Cleaning services was a suitable category to be split by regions, and therefore for creating a framework agreement. Market research was conducted in order to gain knowledge on the specificities relating to cleaning services.

Key suppliers of cleaning services were contacted and their experiences were discussed. This was a mandatory step before starting the demand aggregation, as the officials in charge of the procurement procedure needed to understand how to formulate tables for the demand aggregation, what data to ask for, etc.

The procurement team learned about the classification of space, the types of cleaning services, the percentage of labour in the price of service per m^2, the types of cleaning products used, etc. Information on the current contracts of the cleaning service suppliers was also provided.

The initial market research step led to the understanding that the two major classifications of cleaning services are per type of space and per frequency of cleaning.

Source: Adapted from OECD (2014), *Manual on Framework Agreements*, OECD, Paris.

Regarding the awareness of procurement opportunities, the reason for engaging with suppliers from the very beginning, and in subsequent pre-tendering stages of the framework agreement, is for the dissemination of information on procurement opportunities to the maximum number of suppliers to ensure efficient competition.

In addition to engaging with suppliers, early engagement by the CPB, which acts as an intermediary between the demand and supply side, with contracting authorities is critical for the identification of their needs and specifications in terms of quantity and function-specific quality. The early engagement of contracting authorities also has the benefits of increasing their participation and the use of the framework agreement. For instance, the Public Works and Government Services in Canada has developed various tools to facilitate the early engagement of suppliers and contracting authorities (Box 3.2).

Box 3.2. Early engagement of suppliers and contracting authorities in Canada

The Public Works and Government Services (PWGSC) in Canada encourages in its supply manual early engagement between client departments and potential suppliers to ensure that public tenders meet market capabilities.

Client departments are invited to engage with PWGSC contracting officers early in the process. This engagement may focus on different topics and may include various levels of engagement. It may be long before a signed requisition is received within PWGSC.

The early engagement with industry may also take many forms, such as:

- Issuing Letters of Interest (LOIs)
- Requests for Information (RFIs)

Box 3.2. Early engagement of suppliers and contracting authorities in Canada *(continued)*

- One-on-one consultations with suppliers
- Holding of industry days
- Informal discussions
- Online questionnaires
- Online collaboration tools
- Focus groups

By engaging clients and suppliers through early and ongoing consultation and dialogue, contracting officers are better situated to identify the various complexities and risks associated with a client's requirement, enabling the development of mitigation strategies. Acquiring the knowledge of the requirement, and its related complexities and risks, better positions all stakeholders for a successful procurement that meets the client's needs.

Various tools are available to facilitate this early engagement. For example:

- **The Acquisitions Program Policy Suite**, which provides policy instruments on topics such as engagement and communications, governance, socio-economic objectives and risk management.
- **The Procurement Library**, which includes the Complexity Assessment tools and copies of Risk Assessments for Complexity Levels 1 to 3.
- **The Procurement Nuggets**, which provide quick references on various procurement issues.

Source: OECD (2015a), *Effective Delivery of Large Infrastructure Projects: The Case of the New International Airport of Mexico City*, OECD Public Governance Reviews, OECD Publishing, Paris, http://dx.doi.org/10.1787/9789264248335-en.

The way tender requirements are written can affect the number and type of suppliers attracted to the tender and, therefore, the success of the selection process. How they are written can also affect the number of contracting authorities using the framework agreement when the use of CPB services is not mandatory for all contracting authorities, or when contracting authorities are allowed to not use the framework agreement if they find better conditions outside or if the products and services offered by suppliers do not correspond to their needs. The clearer the requirements, the easier it will be for potential suppliers to understand them and to prepare and submit bids, and for contracting authorities to use the framework agreement.

Designing a framework agreement involves a careful balancing between enhancing competition and reducing the number of qualified suppliers. While a small number of suppliers could be associated with low levels of competition, inefficiency could rise when a large number of suppliers are included under framework agreements. When many actors are involved, suppliers may not give their best offer while submitting the bid because they know they have a good chance to be part of the framework agreement anyway, and because there is likely only a small share of business from the framework agreement. In this regard, the number of economic operators that are part of each framework agreement is a critical point to consider.

Participation in a bid represents a real cost for the economic operators, but also for the CPB and contracting authorities. This is also valid for the second stage competition (the call-off phase) of the framework agreement, since contracting authorities, through the CPB platform, must invite all economic operators under the framework agreement to participate. For this reason, many CPBs and contracting authorities set specific rules to limit the number of suppliers who can be awarded a specific framework agreement.

Decisions on the number of economic operators that are part of a framework agreement depends on the country, the market analysis and the secondary policy objectives to implement, such as the access of small and medium-sized enterprises (SMEs) to public procurement. For instance, Box 3.3 explains how Consip, the Italian central purchasing body, determines the number of suppliers under framework agreements to maximise efficiencies.

Box 3.3. Balancing the number of suppliers for framework agreements: Examples from Consip (Italy)

Consip determines the number of suppliers using a flexible rule that depends on the number of valid tenders received. It balances competition and maximum participation.

Examples of rules in some framework agreements:

Framework agreements	Number of suppliers under the FA
Desktop outsourcing	Valid tenders ≤ 6 => 3 suppliers Valid tenders > 6 => 4 suppliers
Open Source	Valid tenders n => n-1 suppliers (maximum 7)
Travel agency services	Valid tenders ≤ 5 c => 3 suppliers Valid tenders 6-7 => 4 suppliers Valid tenders ≥ 8 => 5 suppliers

This system has enabled a significant increase of savings as suppliers have a strong incentive to be ranked first.

Source: Information provided by Consip.

Depending on the framework agreement and the nature of products and services, CPBs apply specific minimum requirements to ensure the capability of the suppliers to perform the contract. However, suppliers need to be proportional to the size and terms and conditions of the procurement contract. Minimum requirements may be in the form of pre-qualification requirements and capability tests related to the activity of the supplier, such as stock capabilities, robustness of the supply chain, and annual revenues assessed against projected expenditures under the framework agreement. Other requirements relate to legal aspects, such as the fulfilment of legal obligations in terms of taxes and labour conditions.

In some countries, contracting authorities, or the CPB in charge of the framework agreement, require large and disproportionate monetary guarantees or bonds from bidders as a condition for submitting a bid. Bid or participation bonds are the two main types of bonds often demanded to make sure bidding companies execute the contract when it is awarded. The performance bond serves as collateral to ensure that all terms of the contract are respected. As described in the European code of best practices facilitating access by SMEs to public contract (European Commission, 2008), this kind of practice, when used disproportionately, represents an administrative and financial obstacle in terms of competition for some categories of bidders, such as SMEs, since they can have difficulties providing these bonds.

Selecting suppliers with the necessary technical and professional ability to bid for contracts ensures good delivery of public services and value for money. Countries have different ways to assess suppliers' ability to fulfil a contract. For instance, a supplier's technical and professional ability could be demonstrated by its performance of past contracts, as in Korea (Box 3.4). Some countries take the past performance of suppliers into account by excluding them from a framework agreement. Suppliers may be excluded for the following reasons:

- Delays in providing the goods and/or services in accordance with the framework agreement
- Failure to supply all the goods and/or services in accordance with the scope set out in the framework agreement
- Failure to meet any service levels and/or supply the goods and/or services
- Negative feedback from contracting authorities

Box 3.4. Taking account of suppliers' past performance in Korea

Established in 1949 as the Provisional Office of Foreign Supply, the Public Procurement Service (PPS) took on its current role as the central procurement agency of the Republic of Korea in 1961. The mission of the PPS is "To provide the best value service to its clients, save national budget spending and contribute to economic development by procuring and managing resources for public administration."

PPS is responsible for the establishment and management of Korea Multiple Award Schedules (MAS) framework contracts. MAS was designed to meet the differing needs of various end users through contracts awarded to multiple suppliers, each offering goods of similar quality, performance and efficiency. PPS issues unit-price contracts annually with qualified suppliers, who must have an acceptable past delivery performance and satisfactory financial standing. These products and prices are then listed in the Online Shopping Mall, and each end user can make purchases directly, without the need for direct involvement of PPS contracting staff or the issuance of a new contract.

This arrangement provides a number of benefits. First, it provides more options for end users by providing access to a broader range of suppliers. It also allows more suppliers to participate in the public procurement process – as long as the minimum requirements for satisfactory past performance in at least three instances and a credit rating above a certain threshold are satisfied, any supplier can participate. This increased number of suppliers also generates increased competition. Not only do suppliers compete on price, but also on quality of similar product, delivery terms and rated after-sales service, which refers to the suppliers' responsiveness to inquiries, requests for action on defects and other performance elements.

Source: OECD (2016), *The Korean Public Procurement Service: Innovating for Effectiveness*, OECD Public Governance Reviews, OECD Publishing, Paris, http://dx.doi.org/10.1787/9789264249431-en.

Basing contract award decisions on past performance encourages companies to achieve better acquisition outcomes over the long term, and helps ensure that the contracting authority or the CPB will contract with firms that are likely to meet performance expectations. Moreover, under a system that allows for past performance criteria, suppliers compete not only on price but also on quality. However, for past performance information to be useful, it must be documented, relevant, fair and reliable; there also need to be systems, tools and metrics for sharing the information, such as in the United States (Box 3.5).

Box 3.5. Taking account of suppliers' past performance in the United States

Federal agencies are required since July 2009 to post all contractor performance evaluations on the Past Performance Information Retrieval System (PPIRS,). That web-based, government-wide application provides timely and pertinent information on a contractor's past performance to the federal acquisition community for making source selection decisions. PPIRS provides a query capability for authorised users to retrieve report card information detailing a contractor's past performance. Federal regulations require that report cards be completed annually by customers during the life of the contract. The PPIRS consists of several sub-systems and databases (e.g. contractor performance system, past performance data Base, and construction contractor appraisal support system).

Source: OECD (2013), *Colombia: Implementing Good Governance*, OECD Public Governance Reviews, OECD Publishing, Paris, http://dx.doi.org/10.1787/9789264202177-en.

The CPB or contracting authority running a tender need to consider the cost of the bid, as well as the time associated, as this has a great implication on competition and efficiency. The higher the cost of the tender, the lower the level of competition. This is true for framework agreements, but also for call-offs. For this reason, the use of electronic bidding systems and, more generally, e-procurement systems, can be seen as a way to remove barriers to competition as they enable cheap and quick communication. Some economic operators, such as SMEs, do not have large and specialised administrative capacities. Therefore, contracting authorities and CPBs could try to keep administrative requirements to a minimum as a way of enhancing competition.

In terms of processes, there is a strong link between competition and deadlines to submit bids. As such, CPBs and contracting authorities could take into account all constraints of economic operators in order to set an appropriate timeframe to receive more bids and better bids in terms of quality.

The boundaries of a procurement market are essentially defined by the tender specifications. Therefore, careful attention on the tender specifications is necessary to ensure that the market is defined as widely as possible, and that barriers to entry are as low as possible. In procurement markets, barriers to entry can be lowered by designing tender participation criteria that are not unnecessarily restrictive, by allowing firms from other regions or countries to participate, or by devising ways of incentivising smaller firms to participate, even if they cannot bid for the entire contract.

Of key importance for a framework agreement's design is its capability to meet a specific need, not a specific product or service. The standardisation of products and services is the process of homogenisation and setting generally uniform characteristics for a particular good or service that may reduce the variety of products that fall under similar descriptions. This can be a powerful way to increase the efficiency of the framework agreement in terms of competition, and is a big step towards the rationalisation of public spending. The standardisation, and thus the categorisation of products and services under a framework agreement in the system, play a key role in the second-stage competition.

Allowing contracting authorities to choose the categories and sub-categories for call-offs by going further in the technical specification could dramatically decrease competition.

Promoting engagement with suppliers: A shared objective across countries

According to the OECD's survey, CPBs consult suppliers when carrying out market research (92%) and demand analysis (83%). After receiving information and opinions on the needs and the market, suppliers are consulted less often. Half of the countries surveyed engage with suppliers for the general design of the framework agreement.

Figure 3.1. Supplier consultations at different stages of framework agreement preparation

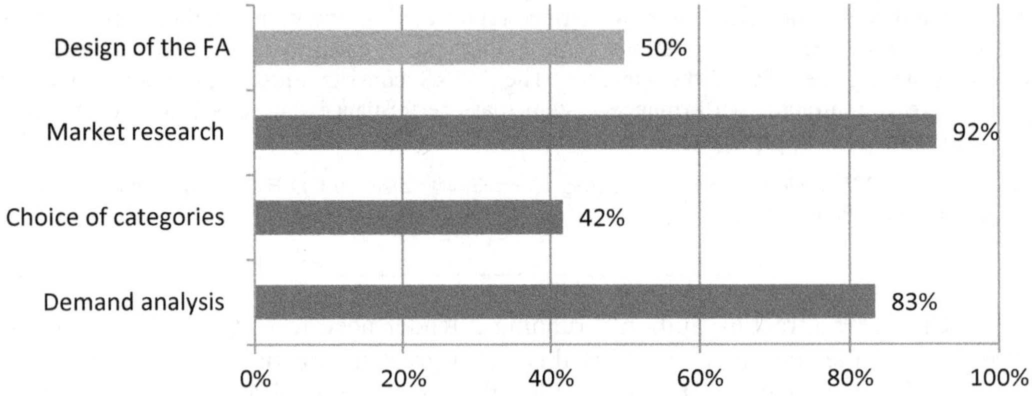

Note: Lighter blue colour indicates where Chile does not take part.

Source: OECD (2015) Survey on Centralised Framework Agreements, OECD Paris.

For instance, in New Zealand, the suppliers are consulted dependent on the market and the requirements: their Strategic engagement methods include public notices, requests for information, "speed dating" sessions, meet the supplier sessions, industry workshops and, if appropriate, one to one engagement.

It is worth noting that most of the CPBs surveyed are European. In their model, the number of suppliers under the framework agreement is considerably smaller than in ChileCompra.

ChileCompra carries out supplier consultations at different preparation stages of framework agreements, notably at the demand analysis stage, the market research and the choice of categories stages which are mainly done through requests for information (RFI).

ChileCompra co-ordinates the Propyme (*Pro Pequena y Mediana Empresas*) committee, which is a consultative body with a clear goal of proposing actions and promoting the activities of ChileCompra in terms of public procurement to SMEs.[1] This committee meets five times per year and is composed of representatives of ChileCompra, industry associations, the Ministry of Economy, chambers of commerce and trade associations. The ChileCompra website has a forum for all relevant actors to share their opinions and perspectives. In the executive summary of the 3rd Propyme committee meeting in September 2013, survey results were shared especially on the reasons for low competition in ChileCompra activities. Reasons included difficulty to access the information, its low circulation, and the lack of the supply and the type of contracts (Figure 3.2).

Figure 3.2. Reasons for low competition in ChileCompra activities

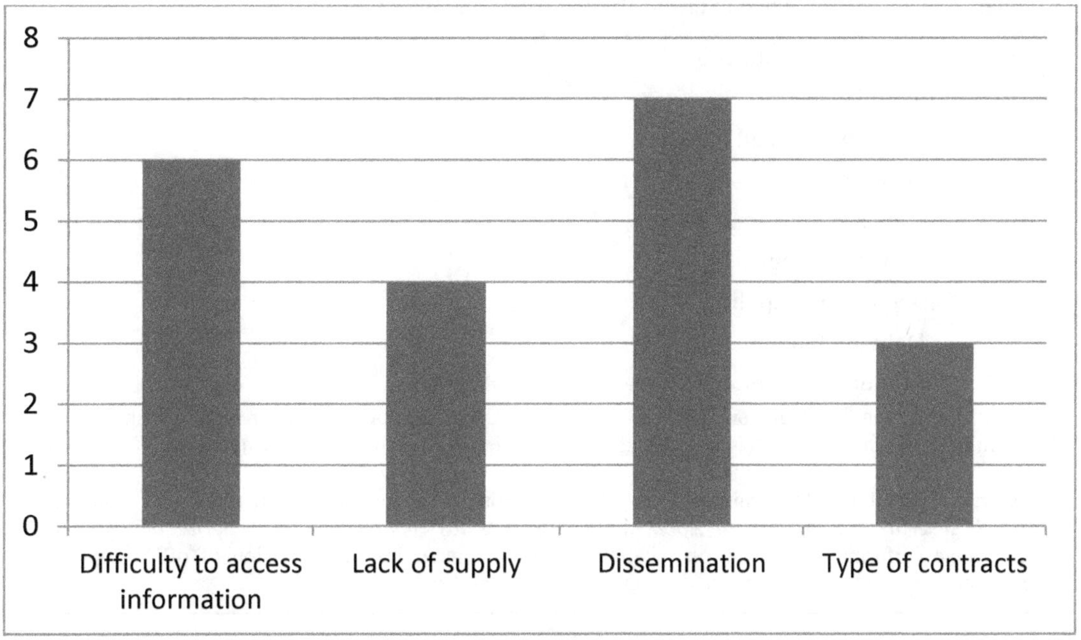

Source: Based on information provided by Chilecompra

Suppliers participate in decisions on the procurement strategy in some countries. For example, they can influence decisions on procurement procedures, such as in France and New Zealand. The extent of their participation in the decision varies across countries, however, the final decisions are made by the CPBs. The participation of suppliers in decisions on the award criteria of the framework agreement exists only in New Zealand and Spain. In Spain, all main lines of procedures are subject to suggestions, including from suppliers through a request of information (Box 3.6).

Box 3.6. Supplier participation in the procurement strategy: Spain

In Spain, the Directorate-General for Rationalisation and Centralisation of Procurement (DGRCC) acts as a CPB for the central administrations. Its main mission is the promotion, management and monitoring of centralised procurement in the state public sector.

For the purposes of increasing the transparency of centralized procurement processes and of ascertaining the views of the business sector to which the framework agreements are directed, the DGRCC holds meetings with business associations and public sessions with potential tenderers and associations during the preparation of the conditions of tender. These sessions allow the DGRCC to get the views of the sector on a diverse range of aspects of procurement. This process concludes, on most occasions, with the distribution of a questionnaire (RFI) for the companies and associations to give their opinion on the different aspects of the procurement approach.

Box 3.6. Supplier participation in the procurement strategy: Spain *(continued)*

For instance, after an open meeting on the future framework agreement on office suppliers, suppliers and associations had to answer a questionnaire on the:

- Duration of the contract
- Scope of the contract
  - Availability of all products? If not why?
  - Quality
  - Packages
- Delivery zones/regions
- Management of supplies:
  - Delivery times
  - Minimum orders

Sources: Directorate-General for Rationalization and Centralization of Procurement's website (n.d.), "Consulting companies," http://contratacioncentralizada.gob.es/consultasaempresas (Accessed 1st February 2016).

Directorate-General for Rationalization and Centralization of Procurement (2015),*"Jornada Informativa sobre el Acuerdo Marco para la Adopción de Tipo de los Suministros de Material de Oficina no* Inventariable (Informative session on the framework agreement for the provision of office supplies)", http://catalogocentralizado.minhap.es/pctw/Documentos/AM_MONI.pdf.

Box 3.7. Engaging with suppliers in Portugal

The National Agency for Public Procurement in Portugal (ESPAP) conducts two types of consultations to engage suppliers:

1. A public consultation where the CPB presents the tender purposes and specifications. The main aim is to gather feedback from all relevant stakeholders, such as suppliers. During this consultation, ESPAP clearly describes the:
   - Objectives of the agency and framework agreements (general)
   - Type of procedure, duration, lots and set-up of the framework agreements
   - Awarding criteria and proposals ranking
   - Minimum technical and functional requirements (base + optional)
   - Conditions to participate in the tender
   - Product update and changes in the offer during the framework agreements
2. A preliminary consultation, which is an informal consultation with future interested parties (economic operators), can be accepted for procedure preparation and information purposes. This process could result in recommendations or relevant market information being issued. Special attention on competition protection and non-discrimination and transparency principles is required.

Source: based on a presentation given at a workshop supporting the Greek public procurement reform, June 2014.

The publication of a prior information notice to make suppliers aware of upcoming procurement opportunities is generally regarded as best practice. There is no specific rule or timeline to publish the notice. It is published in several countries with different timeframes: 2-11 months before the tender invitation in Belgium; 6-8 months before in Finland, except for very few procedures; and 3-4 months before in Spain, through a web portal. In Italy, the notice is published during the very early stages of market consultation. In New Zealand, prior information notices are posted on GETS (Government Electronic Tendering Service), and upcoming opportunities are posted on the New Zealand Government Procurement (NZGP) website, including annual procurement plans.

ChileCompra does not publish any prior information notice, and the information related to the framework agreement is only available in the tender publication stage.

As a specific procurement instrument, the implementation of framework agreements requires tailored procurement processes

ChileCompra could further engage with suppliers and contracting authorities to enhance competition

Establishing an ongoing dialogue between industries, contracting authorities and the CPB throughout the procurement process should begin as early as the needs identification stage. Early engagement mitigates risks, identifies innovative solutions, and enhances competition by connecting buyers and suppliers early on in the process.

ChileCompra's co-ordination of the Propyme Committee is a good initiative to promote early engagement. However, this committee is intended only for SMEs, which represent less than 50% of procurement value and purchase orders. In order to create an environment that is conducive to competition, the first step for ChileCompra is to invite all interested suppliers from all categories to a dialogue with the procuring agency on the technical and administrative specifications of the procurement opportunity, or on the framework agreement more generally.

Figure 3.3. Share of companies by their size in terms of value and number of purchase orders in Chile

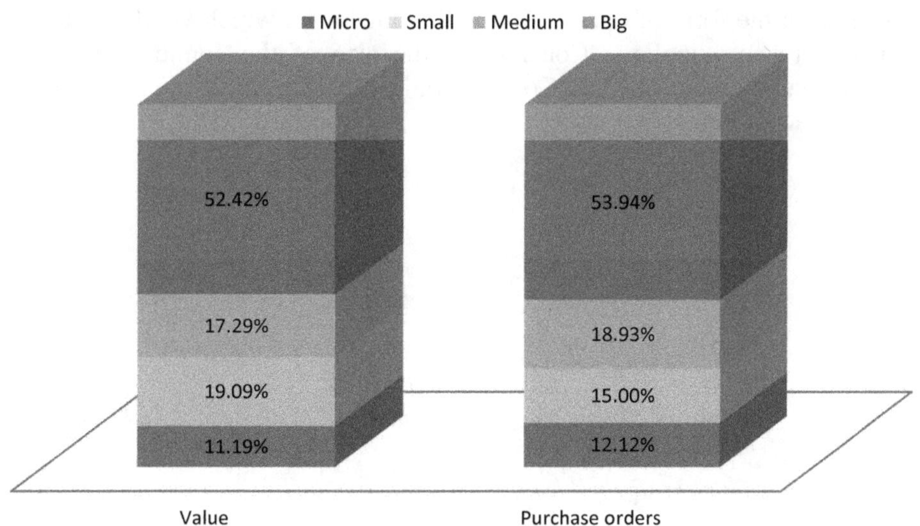

Source: Information provided by Chilecompra.

Instituting clear processes and actions at different stages using various means is critical for enabling ChileCompra to unlock the benefits of the early engagement of suppliers. The publication of procurement plans is considered as a good practice to inform suppliers at a very early stage. Various CPBs publish procurement plans based on demand analysis, but also on the exact end time of a framework agreement. The best option to reach out to the broadest audience is to publish procurement plans on the CPB website or the national procurement website. This gives a clear visibility to suppliers on the upcoming opportunities in the medium to long term. On the ChileCompra website,[2] the annual plan of procurement is currently available on previous years where this information is crucial for the upcoming years to help the suppliers. A regular update of the information available in the website is a key factor of success.

In some countries, any contracting authority or CPB can publish a prior information notice that describes the amount, and sometimes the characteristics, of tenders to be launched in the next twelve months. This enables economic operators to be aware of, and prepared for, future procurement opportunities in the middle term. For instance, the European Commission provides an advanced and complete model[3] of the prior information notice. On the ChileCompra website,[4] suppliers can see the upcoming framework agreements for 2016. However, the information provided is minimal and describes only the procurement area, it does not adequately enable suppliers to prepare to submit bids. Providing more information, including a short description of the nature and quantities of the framework agreement or the scope of works, the scheduled date for start of award procedures and the duration of the contract, would enable ChileCompra to raise the awareness of future opportunities among its supplier community.

The introduction of requests for information before the publication of a framework agreement is considered as good practice to enable a better design of the tender specifications. RFIs are distinct from requests for quotation (RFQ)s: RFIs address issues related to tender design and specification in general, whereas RFQs are mainly intended to get prices. Using all components of RFIs for all tenders could help ChileCompra have a better understanding of each market.

ChileCompra could also institutionalise meetings with suppliers before the launch of each framework agreement in order to ensure more engagement from the supply side. These could be in the form of open or individual meetings, which would ensure equality of treatment between suppliers. Considering the size of the country and the risk of collusion when suppliers meet, ChileCompra could consider online open meetings to help reduce face-to-face interaction.

Box 3.8. Industry days in Canada

Canada uses the smart procurement approach of early engagement to ask suppliers for their expertise before a requirement is identified. This is achieved through an increased number of industry days, one-on-one supplier consultations, and other engagement activities.

For instance, the Department of National Defence, Canadian Forces Base, Edmonton, Alberta, has a requirement for the provision of television services that includes the media, labour, material, supervision, equipment and transportation necessary to fulfill this requirement. Television media could include those provided through cable (fibre or copper); radio frequency, such as satellite or microwave; or Internet protocol streaming over the Internet.

Because of the complex nature of the requirement, the contracting authorities organised an "industry day" with industry representatives to discuss this requirement in detail. The purpose of this session was to proactively communicate the government's intent to purchase television services, and, as a stakeholder, suppliers had the opportunity to bring forward suggestions to make the process effective, efficient, and aligned with industry practices.

Source: Public Works and Government Services Canada (n.d.). "Benefits of Smart Procurement." https://buyandsell.gc.ca/initiatives-and-programs/smart-procurement/benefits-of-smart-procurement.

Reaching all suppliers individually can be difficult, and RFIs through the ChileCompra website may not be a sufficient way of reaching suppliers and collecting valuable information. It is therefore essential for ChileCompra to keep working actively with other institutions, such as:

- Industry associations that can be used as legitimate, pro-competitive mechanisms for members of a procurement sector to promote standards and competition.
- Chambers of commerce, whose goal is to further the interests of businesses.

Both types of institution can provide valuable information on the market, and also act effectively to relay information to their members, and thus enhance competition. ChileCompra has established links with these institutions through the Propyme committee. However, the key is to ensure that the information is then transmitted to suppliers with clear action plans and follow-ups. ChileCompra could consider establishing relationships outside the Propyme committee for each procurement area.

For ChileCompra's framework agreements, suppliers have two months to submit a bid. ChileCompra should consider adapting the procurement process to each framework agreement, depending on the procurement area and the complexity of the framework agreement. While ensuring suppliers have adequate time to submit their bids, the early engagement of suppliers can enable a reduction of the timeline, since suppliers could be made aware of and prepared for procurement opportunities.

Chilecompra could further develop subject matter expertise according to product categories

In terms of the efficiency of the framework agreement, category managers or subject matter experts play a significant role. In some CPBs, category managers should at least be specialised at the procurement area level as they need a good knowledge of a specific market and its environment. Category managers should know the industrial sector in which they operate, market trends, products and services available in the market, and all the other relevant information necessary for a good understanding of the market and a decrease of information asymmetry. These tasks should be undertaken during the preparation of the tender, but also during the entire tender life. Even if those tasks are more demanding in terms of time, the impact in terms of competition and efficiency will be much more significant.

The inclusion of appropriate subject matter experts in the design of the tender specification could lead to a further rationalisation of the offering and the pool of suppliers.

Figure 3.4. Share of products transacted

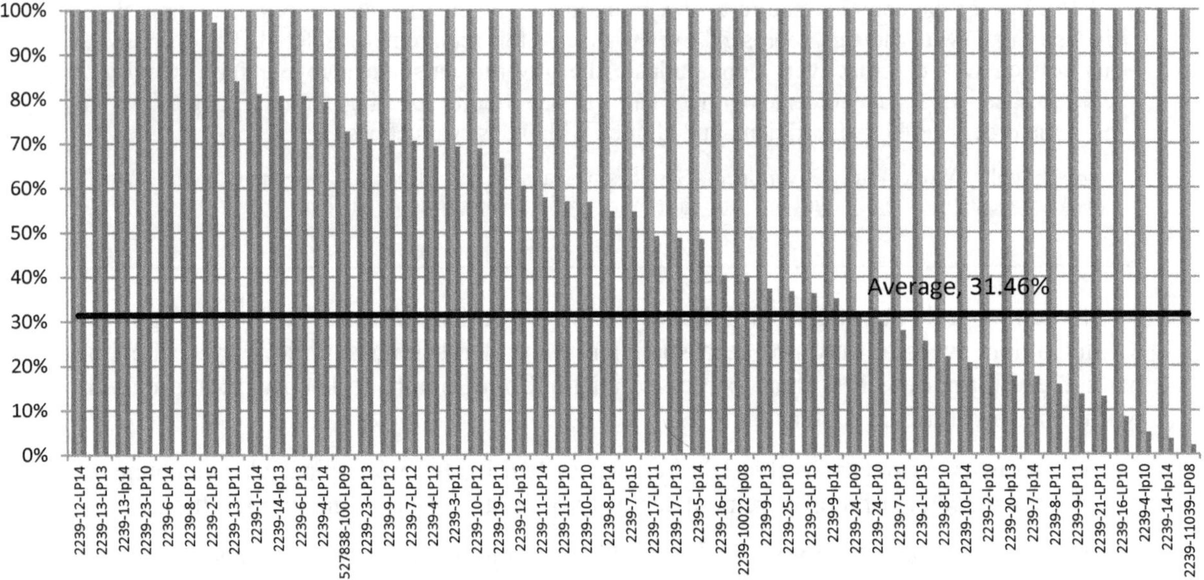

Source: OECD analysis based on information provided by Chilecompra

Indeed, only 31.5% of the products included in the platform are effectively transacted. This represents a waste of time and a cost for the CPB, but also for suppliers. Hence, to reduce the time spent on the design of the tender specification, and on the checking and update of products and services, a further development of procurement expertise could help when selecting the relevant products and services to include in the framework agreement and in the platform, and would allow for a greater focus by category managers on strategic decisions.

In the case of a new framework agreement, in-house expertise developed as early as possible would help in understanding the relevant market challenges. An example of this in Chile is the experience of ChileCompra with medical devices. ChileCompra established a strategic alliance with the Institute of Public Health (*Instituto de Salud Pública*) and received feedback from two main contracting authorities: San Juan Hospital and the Hospital of Chile University. For this framework agreement, the average percentage of transacted products is high (around 85%) compared to those in other framework agreements of ChileCompra. It clearly supports the positive impacts of this kind of alliances and the benefits of early engagement with the contracting authorities which would be essential for Chilecompra to establish in other procurement areas.

The standardisation of goods and services is crucial for enhancing competition and increasing efficiency

The standardisation of products and services, while ensuring the market is defined as widely as possible in the tender specification, can enhance the efficiency of the system and boost competition in the market. Tenders should reflect the diversity of the technical solutions available in the marketplace, with certain limits. The easier a product/service can be standardised, the higher the chance to aggregate the volume, the value of the framework agreement, and thus the savings.

Information available on the platform regarding the use of products and services would be a valuable input for ChileCompra when deciding which products and services to be included in the framework agreement. From the products and services managed by ChileCompra, only 39.8% had more than one purchase order, and 12% were disqualified or not available. When renewing a framework agreement it is essential for ChileCompra to consider whether or not to include the products and services that are never or rarely ordered. This analysis can help to define standardised products and services.

Figure 3.5. Percentage of products having received 0 or 1 purchase order

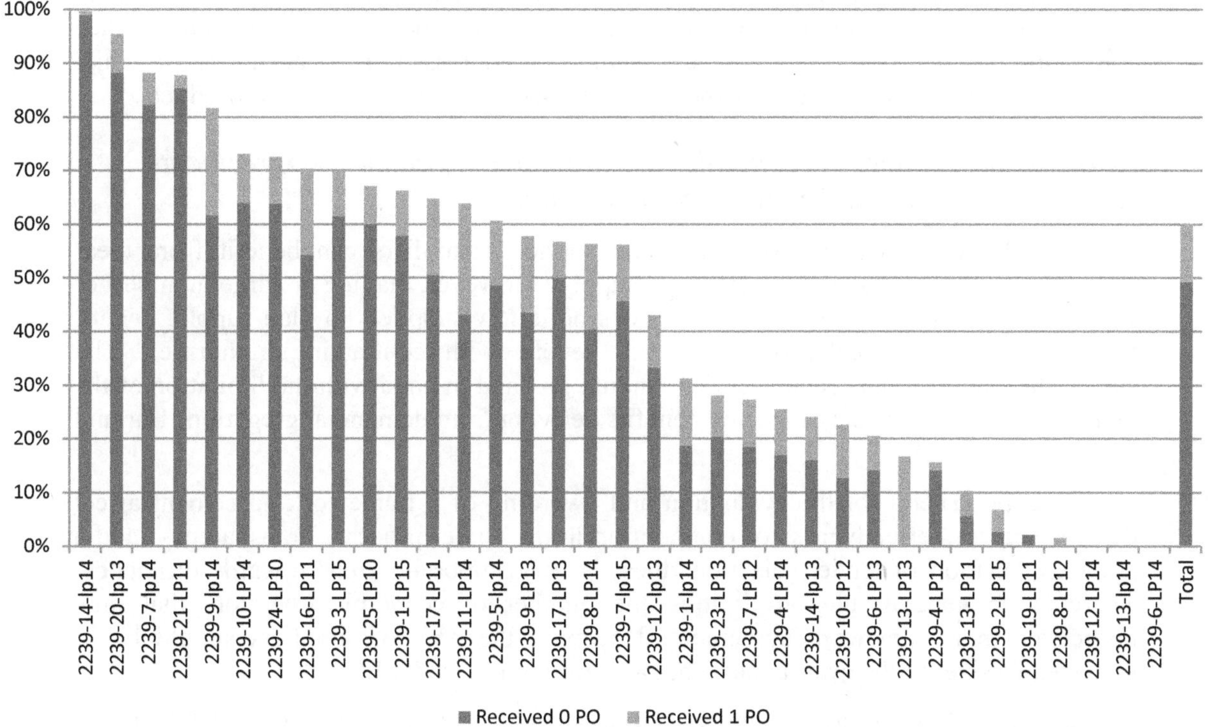

Source: OECD analysis based on information provided by Chilecompra

Defining specifications as widely as possible would enhance the efficiency of the system, as going into high specifications and details, such as the SKU (stock keeping unit) level, would reduce competition. This work is directly linked with the standardisation and categorisation established by the CPB. For example, in ChileCompra there are 28 different categories of rice and even more subcategories.

Categories are sometimes duplicated or very similar. This way of categorisation could lead to reduced competition, especially for procurement above the threshold. Categories should reflect the tender specifications, which means products and services meeting the need, not a wide and detailed description of the products and services to be procured.

Contracting authorities are obliged to use ChileCompra framework agreements unless they find better conditions outside, and data on framework agreement coverage clearly shows that the average coverage is quite low (59.3%). This means that more than one third of the amount spent by contracting authorities, for which a framework agreement is available, is spent on goods/services outside the framework agreement.

A smart standardisation of products and services gives a clear visibility to suppliers on the real demand side. It can lead to increased competition among suppliers, as all will compete for the same standardised products and services. This will increase the efficiency of the framework agreement and increase its coverage. This process is crucial for ChileCompra since it impacts the efficiency of public spending, but also the sustainability of the model.

Standardisation also allows for meaningful price comparison. Currently, ChileCompra Express (the electronic procurement platform) allows contracting authorities to filter by price, but not by price per unit. The price per unit would constitute relevant information to be displayed in order to make comparison possible and enhance competition among suppliers. This issue should be addressed at the design phase while imposing to suppliers in the tender specifications specific units and sizes of products.

Reducing the number of economic operators under framework agreements could help Chile to further promote competition

With the standardisation of goods and services, suppliers can benefit from clear visibility of the goods and services to supply. However, having a large number of suppliers under a framework agreement does not allow suppliers to plan supply, benefit from economies of scale, or share this benefit with contracting authorities. The standardisation of products and services should go hand in hand with the limitation of the number of suppliers to maximise the benefits deriving from demand aggregation (Harland et al., 1999).

Selection criteria for the evaluation and awarding of a framework agreement affect the intensity and effectiveness of competition in the tender process. Transparency, and a good explanation of tender selection rules, is very important steps towards efficiency. There is no general rule on limiting the number of economic operators that may participate in a framework agreement. However, the pool of suppliers should be of manageable size for the award phase, but also during the tender life.

For the framework agreements available in 2015, ChileCompra received 8 209 bids and awarded 6 004 of them. This means that ChileCompra had to analyse a significant number of bids, for which nearly one third were not awarded. The evaluation phase (including the qualification of suppliers) takes between two to eight months which is understandable given the high number of suppliers. However, a long evaluation phase increases the risk that bids awarded are not up-to-date in terms of price or needs.

SMEs account for 90% of suppliers under ChileCompra's procurement system, but they represent only 47.6% in terms of value, and 46% in terms of the number of purchase orders. Around 60% of suppliers under framework agreements in 2014 had no transactions in the same year. This could mean that a large range of suppliers and SMEs do not receive any orders, or receive only a few. This implies inefficiencies in the system for a wide range of suppliers, particularly when considering the costliness of the bidding process. Hence, the CPB should carefully assess the market, their requirements and resources during the preparation stage, and decide on the appropriate number of economic operators for each framework agreement.

The number of suppliers under a framework agreement ranges from 1 to 1 094, with an average of 147. The mechanism does not encourage suppliers to give their best offer as they know they have a good chance of being part of the framework agreement anyway. For procurement under the threshold, contracting authorities can buy from any supplier without having complete information on the initial selection phase, such as the ranking of suppliers. ChileCompra could consider introducing a mechanism to make visible the ranking of suppliers and to give a larger share to those ranked higher. This could incentivise suppliers to give a more competitive price. This mechanism will reduce the information gap as ranking is not only based on the price criterion and thus will enhance competition and likely decrease prices.

The capability tests of suppliers checked by ChileCompra are minimal as the CPB generally only checks the fulfilment of legal obligations (taxes, labour conditions, etc.). This could explain the high number of bids, the low percentage of disqualified suppliers (4%), and the high percentage of products not available (11%). To strengthen the quality of suppliers, ChileCompra should consider the introduction of a prequalification stage and additional capability tests, such as stock capability or the robustness of the supply chain, depending on the procurement area.

A good way to ensure the quality of suppliers is to introduce past performance criterion, which is used for some tenders by ChileCompra. However, to use this criterion efficiently, the CPB should not ask only about years or numbers of experience in the specific procurement area but also information related to the quality of suppliers in the performance of previous contracts. This information should be documented, relevant and reliable, and adapted to each procurement area. ChileCompra should consider developing a system or a platform to receive feedback from contracting authorities on the performance of suppliers regarding the compliance of the contractual clauses (e.g. prices and delays).

To limit the risks related to the performance of the contracts, Chilecompra can ask for various types of guarantees/bonds. The CPB has published instructions on its website[5] on how to use these guarantees:

- Bid bonds are expressed in total value but cannot represent more than 5% of the contract. ChileCompra advises contracting authorities to not ask for those guarantees under the threshold (1 000 UTM[6]), and the CPB should monitor their use.
- Performance bonds are expressed in total value ranging from 5 to 30% of the contract. The percentage to apply will depend on the risk assessment of the procurement.

Limiting the number of economic operators with adequate capability tests can limit the risks related to the performance of procurement, and thus decrease the percentage of the bid and performance bonds. A decrease of financial guarantees according to supplier performance of the contract should be encouraged.

The good design of tenders should not restrict some groups, such as SMEs, from submitting bids for a framework agreement. ChileCompra should allow contracts to be awarded in the form of separate lots when possible. Allotment can be used from a regional perspective, but also for special categories of products and services. The sub-division of public purchases into lots clearly facilitates access by SMEs, both quantitatively (since the size of the lots may better correspond to the productive capacity of the SME) and qualitatively (the content of the lots may correspond more closely to the specialised sector of the SME).

In many countries, such as those under the EU directive, contracting authorities are obliged by law to accept a group of suppliers submitting a bid. In this case, the group or consortium may rely on the capacities of all participants. From the information available, ChileCompra does not currently allow for this kind of co-operation among suppliers, even for the second stage competition. While rationalising the number of suppliers, ChileCompra could consider allowing the grouping of suppliers in order to further remove barriers to participatation.

ChileCompra allows subcontracting for only a small portion of framework agreements, and it is acknowledged that economic operators would prefer to win the entire contract. However, in the case of large contracts, or when there are no SMEs in the market, subcontracting may still provide firms and SMEs opportunities to have a share of the contract through participation in the procurement supply chain. This is particularly the case when SMEs can provide added value in the form of specialised or innovative products or services. In this regard, increasing subcontracting opportunities could further facilitate SME participation in framework agreements.

Notes

1 In Chile, Law N° 20.416 establishes the criteria to define the size of a firm. SMEs are considered as firms with fewer than 200 employees and with an annual turnover up to 100 000 UF (Unidad de Fomento, a unit of account that is adjusted to inflation). It corresponded to USD 3 700 000 in January 2016.

2 Accessible at www.mercadopublico.cl/Home/PlanDeCompra.

3 Accessible at http://simap.ted.europa.eu/documents/10184/49059/sf_001_en.pdf.

4 Accessible at www.mercadopublico.cl/Home/Contenidos/QueEsCM.

5 Accessible at www.mercadopublico.cl/portal/mp2/descargables/Directiva_N_7_Garantias.pdf.

6 UTM (unidad tributaria mensual) is a unit of account in Chile, generally used to calculate taxes, fines and custom duties.

References

Directorate-General for Rationalization and Centralization of Procurement's website (n.d.), "Consulting companies," http://contratacioncentralizada.gob.es/consultasaempresas, (Accessed 1st February 2016).

Directorate-General for Rationalization and Centralization of Procurement (2015). "*Jornada Informativa sobre el Acuerdo Marco para la Adopción de Tipo de los Suministros de Material de Oficina no Inventariable* (Informative session on the framework agreement for the provision of office supplies)", http://catalogocentralizado.minhap.es/pctw/Documentos/AM_MONI.pdf.

European Commission (2008), *European code of best practices facilitating access by SMEs to public procurement contracts*, European Commission, Brussels.

Harland, Lamming and Cousins (1999), *Developing the concept of supply strategy*, International Journal of Operations & Production Management.

OECD (2016), *The Korean Public Procurement Service: Innovating for Effectiveness*, OECD Public Governance Reviews, OECD Publishing, Paris, http://dx.doi.org/10.1787/9789264249431-en.

OECD (2015a), *Effective Delivery of Large Infrastructure Projects: The Case of the New International Airport of Mexico City*, OECD Public Governance Reviews, OECD Publishing, Paris, http://dx.doi.org/10.1787/9789264248335-en.

OECD (2015b), *Survey on Centralised Framework Agreements*, OECD, Paris.

OECD (2014), *Manual on Framework Agreements*, OECD, Paris.

OECD (2013), *Colombia: Implementing Good Governance*, OECD Public Governance Reviews, OECD Publishing, Paris, http://dx.doi.org/10.1787/9789264202177-en.

Public Works and Government Services Canada (n.d.). "Benefits of Smart Procurement." https://buyandsell.gc.ca/initiatives-and-programs/smart-procurement/benefits-of-smart-procurement.

Chapter 4.

Strategic practices for the effective use of framework agreements in Chile

Once implemented by central purchasing bodies (CPBs), framework agreements are meant to be used autonomously by contracting authorities. However, without guidance or structured ordering processes, the potential efficiencies in the tendering process and the selection of suppliers could be put at risk. This chapter assesses country practices in supporting contracting authorities to make the most of existing framework agreements. It provides recommendations for ChileCompra on increasing the efficiency of the system and allowing contracting authorities to take informed purchasing decisions.

A structured call-off stage supported by detailed guidance could boost competition

The award of framework agreements to suppliers does not end ChileCompra's responsibilities and strategic oversight. As for any central purchasing body, the award of framework agreements to suppliers entails follow-up efforts to ensure that the instrument correctly allows for the matching of public entities' needs with market capabilities, while maintaining effective competition.

The use of framework agreements, and the corresponding support provided to both the demand and supply sides, depends on whether a contract already existed or if a new instrument is being implemented. Support during the initiation phase is highly dependent on this factor. Information about the range of products and associated services available under a new framework agreement is essential for ensuring that its coverage is adequately understood.

The classification of information on the products and services available under a framework agreement is a crucial step for ensuring the strategic use of the framework. This information frames the level and structure of the competition at the call-off stage. An extended products typology would allow the end-user to identify those closest to its needs, however, it would also diminish the level of potential competition among qualified suppliers.

Product typology also affects the experience of end-users in processing orders on the platform. Non-intuitive product classification makes the search and identification of offerings that match end-users' needs difficult and longer. This has a direct consequence on the processing costs relating to purchase orders, and therefore on the overarching equilibrium of the framework agreement.

For businesses, extended product typology would open the door to unnecessary product differentiation and result in duplications when either requesting or updating their catalogue. In many countries where a shopping mall of products available under framework agreements is implemented, product updates are supervised by the central purchasing body to ensure relevant product categorisation.

To ensure that requests for modifications are sustainable over time, the majority of respondents to the OECD's survey indicated minimum periods during which changes are not authorised. This is not the case in Chile. In addition, almost half of the countries defined a structured environment for the modification of offerings, whereby suppliers are allocated a maximum number of changes or requests for changes. These practices can mitigate the level of effort and resources needed in the CPB.

The call-off stage, which implies having recourse to another round of competition, commonly exists for purchases above a specified threshold and/or where a detailed and ad-hoc description of the needs of the contracting authority is required. Besides being compulsory to ensure competition among awarded suppliers, second stage competition could also foster the strategic use of framework agreements, provided that the CPB offers appropriate support and guidance. This stage often conveys broader principles relating to strategic procurement, such as need specifications or award criteria, which were applied by skilled and professional procurement officials in the first competition stage.

This exercise in the second stage is carried out by officials with heterogeneous procurement skills, depending on the frequency of their purchasing activities and on their complexity. In New Zealand, the Ministry for Business, Innovation and Employment defined a Procurement Capability Index that aimed to assess the procurement maturity of purchasing agencies (see Annex E). This index allows for a greater and more strategic understanding of support needs, notably in the field of commercial acumen. Guidance and support provided by the central purchasing body during this phase is a major step towards enhancing the strategic use of framework agreements. These efforts could take the form of either real-time assistance via call centres, or supporting documentation and guidance provided online.

For call-offs where second stage competition is not needed, another way of fostering the strategic use of framework agreements is to identify and disclose information on suppliers relating to their initial assessment in the award phase. In many countries, framework agreements are awarded on the basis of a combination of technical and financial assessments. Informing contracting authorities of the outcomes of these assessments would allow them to make an informed decision before issuing an order to a supplier.

This could also affect the behaviour of the supply side in framework agreements, as end-users would have more visibility on the outcomes of the initial tender process. Disclosure could also incentivise suppliers to compete more fiercely in the first competition stage, as they know that the ranking of the initial proposal would affect the potential revenue generated with the framework agreement.

The flexibility of framework agreements, and the options they offer, call for structured support from central purchasing bodies

Supporting contracting authorities and suppliers during the initiation period of framework agreements helps to create a structured environment, which provides stakeholders with a greater understanding of the instruments' main characteristics. For example, a framework agreement that provides specific products and associated services would warrant additional guidance to contracting authorities so that they can maximise their purchasing power by integrating all required goods and services into the same order from the outset. As shown in Figure 4.1, targeted information and support are provided in the initiation phase in order to raise awareness about the existence and structure of recently implemented framework agreements.

Figure 4.1. Steps taken during the initiation of framework agreements

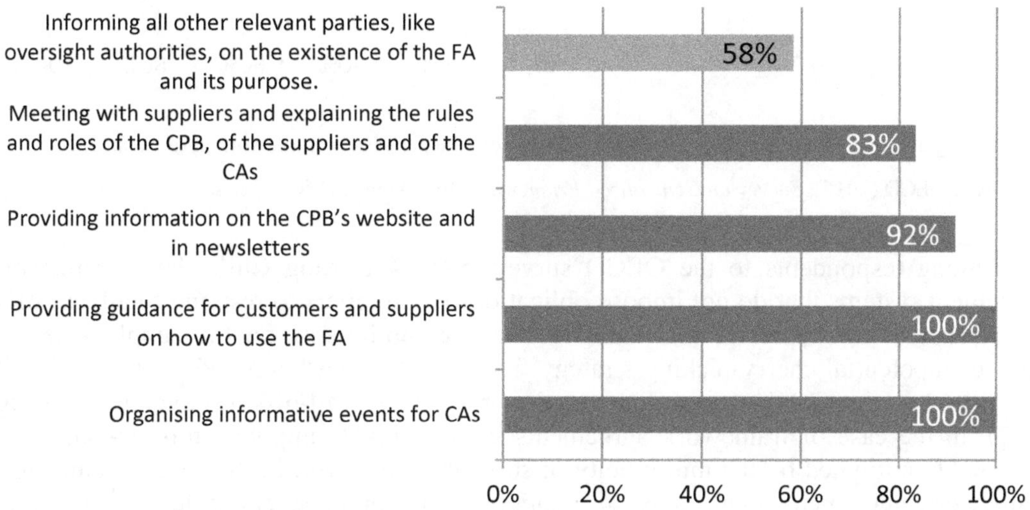

Note: Lighter blue colour indicates where Chile does not take part. FA = framework agreement; CA = contracting authority.

Source: OECD (2015), *Survey on Centralised Framework Agreements*, OECD Paris.

While all respondents to the OECD survey indicated that they provide guidance and information to contracting authorities and suppliers on the use of framework agreements, countries adopt different strategies on the content and format of this support. For example, Consip, the central purchasing body of Italy, takes a proactive approach by providing information relating to framework agreements during the preparation stage in advance of the issuance of the corresponding call for tenders.

ChileCompra has a dedicated Users Division (*Division Servicio al Usarios*) that provides help-desk services and training services to both contracting authorities and suppliers. In 2015, the help-desk received more than 150 000 requests, out of which 69% came from contracting authorities. Among these requests, 15% related to administrative issues, such as forgotten password for accessing ChileCompra Express. Efforts required to address these purely operational requests are absorbing time and resources not allocated to the provision of substantive guidance.

Beyond administrative support, guidance for contracting authorities regarding call-offs imply that second stage competition is further developed in some countries. For example, Finland developed templates to be used by contracting authorities in order to ensure that major procurement principles, such as fairness and transparency, are also followed during this stage.

Figure 4.2. Requirements at the call-off stage

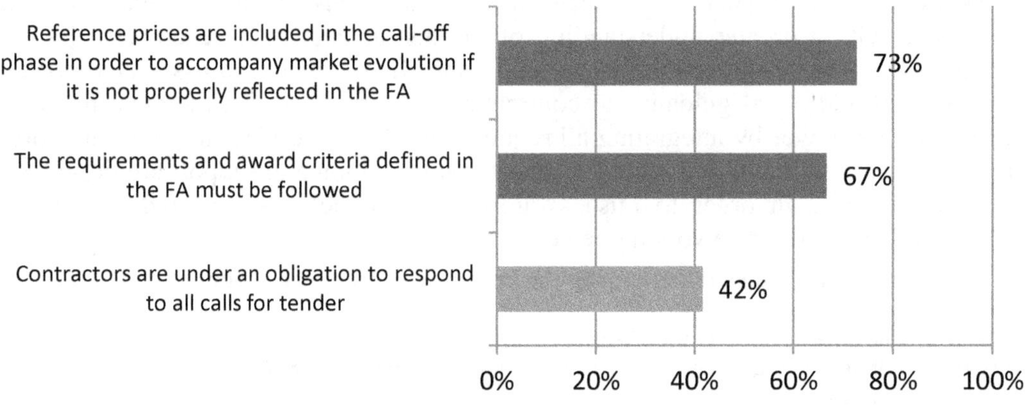

Note: Lighter blue colour indicates where Chile does not take part. FA = framework agreement.

Source: OECD (2015), *Survey on Centralised Framework Agreements*, OECD Paris.

Among respondents to the OECD survey, 58%, including Chile, have framework agreement systems that do not impose obligations on suppliers to respond to all call-offs. As discussed in Chapter 2, this indicates weak commitments on the supply side and induces a potential cherry-picking strategy from suppliers (Albano and Nicholas, 2016). In Chile, less than 19% of awarded suppliers respond to call-offs, on average (see Fig. 4.52). In the case of framework agreements with multiple suppliers, this risk could be reasonably mitigated by the multiplicity of suppliers. However, in the case of mandatory framework agreements with only one supplier, this practice could lead to potential disruption of supply.

Among survey respondents, 73% provide reference prices in the call-off stage to accompany market evolution. This practice helps ensure that prices proposed by suppliers during the mini competition are aligned with the most recent evolution of market prices, irrespective of the date of implementation of the framework agreement.

Figure 4.3. Discounts foreseen in second-stage competition

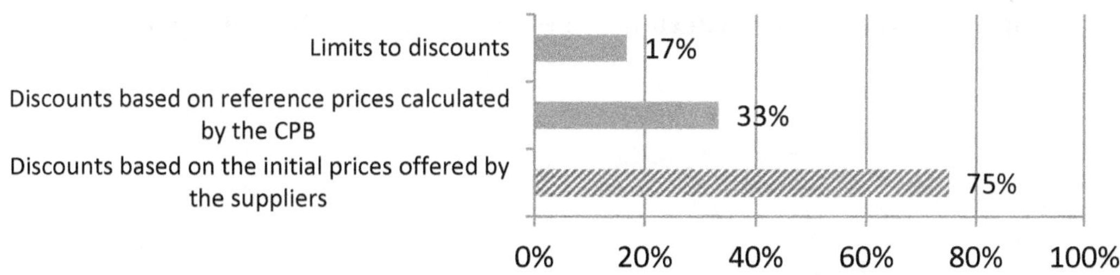

Note: Lighter blue colour indicates where Chile does not take part. Bar with diagonal filling indicates where it is only applicable to some framework agreements in Chile.

Source: OECD (2015), *Survey on Centralised Framework Agreements*, OECD Paris.

Three quarters of survey respondents indicated that discounts obtained during the second stage of the competition are based on the initial prices proposed by suppliers through their first submission, upon which they were awarded the framework agreement. This practice illustrates a rationale whereby the initial prices serve as a competition starting point during the mini competition. It also sets the ground for the measurement of hard savings achieved via the issuance of second stage competition.

Ways that ChileCompra can streamline the use of framework agreements

One a framework agreement has been awarded, central purchasing bodies should ensure that contracting authorities use it to pursue efforts towards efficiencies that were initiated in the design and the open competition stage. To do this, central purchasing bodies could primarily attempt to provide a structured purchasing environment and sufficient guidance to contracting authorities to avoid behaviours and patterns that would harm the efforts achieved in the first stage.

ChileCompra could revisit product categorisation to boost competition and ease ordering process

More than 115 000 products and services are available on ChileCompra Express under 35 distinct framework agreements. However, this does not necessarily mean that there is competition among suppliers of goods and services. Almost half of the products available are only proposed by one supplier inside a given framework agreement, a situation which inherently removes any competition. (Figure 4.4)

On average, products and services are proposed by approximately five suppliers, which tends to indicate an effective level of competition (with the exception of the limitation mentioned above). While this number should illustrate the competitiveness of the offering proposed to contracting authorities, this is not always the case, for example, some product categories comprise up to 850 suppliers.

When looking at the median, analysis shows that only two suppliers are able to compete within the same product category (Figure 4.4). This suggests that a significant number of product categories are not able to attract a sufficient number of bidders, notably in the second stage competition. In the United States, second stage competitions in Multiple Award Schedules (MAS) are required to comprise at least three suppliers to ensure a reasonable degree of competition.

Figure 4.4. Number of products provided by different numbers of suppliers

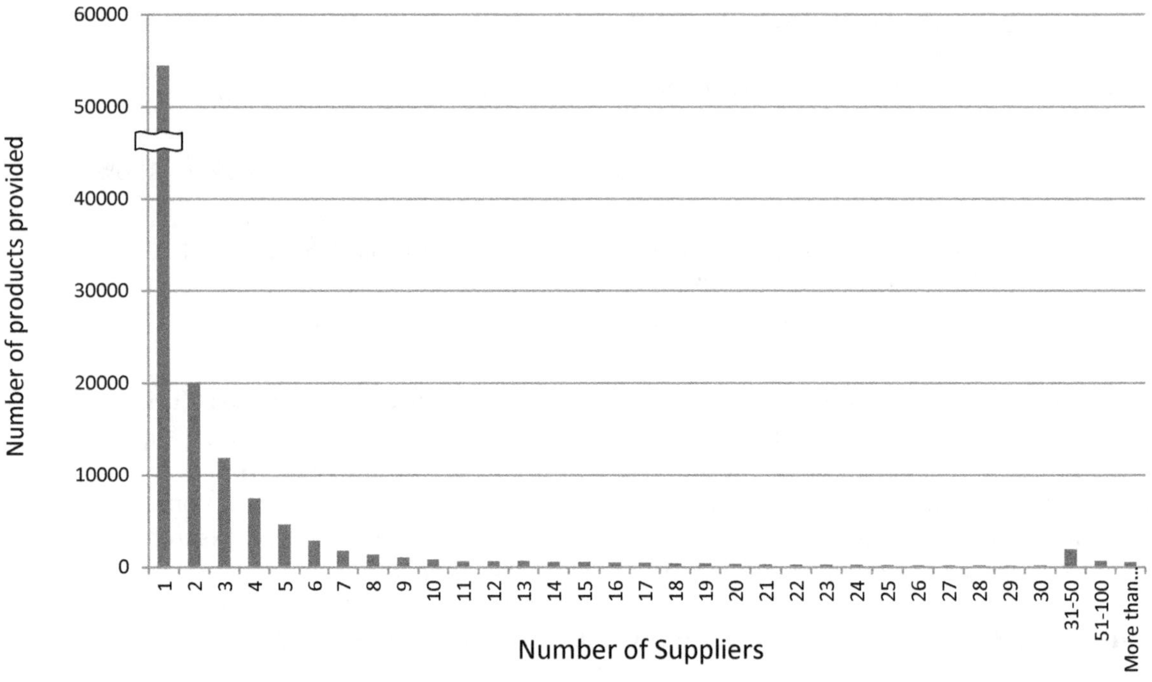

Note: Calculated based on the 117 390 product descriptions database provided by ChileCompra.

Source: OECD analysis based on information provided by ChileCompra.

A low number of potential competitors also renders competition more predictable, which could open the door to bid-rigging practices, such as in Mexico with the Mexican Institute of Social Security (*Instituto Mexicano del Seguro Social* – IMSS), where drugs and medicines public procurement markets were distributed across a small number of main suppliers who collusively agreed to share the market (OECD, 2013).

By rethinking product categorisation, ChileCompra could streamline the ordering process and foster competition among suppliers. This would facilitate contracting authorities' ordering processes by eliminating unnecessary level of details when describing their needs, and as a result provide end-users with a greater number of possible goods and services that match their needs. If adequately categorised and displayed on the platform, the resulting variety of offerings could propose alternatives to end-users that would help them make informed purchasing decisions that go beyond merely comparing financial aspects. Goods and services under the same product category could, for example, be regrouped according to the scoring of the suppliers' proposals against other criteria defined in the call for tender.

In Korean framework agreement systems, innovative (excellence programme) goods and services are identified in the platform so that end-users can decide to purchase them, even if competing products from other suppliers might turn out to be cheaper. Other countries specifically identify goods and services that perform best environmentally. Acting as filters, these selection capabilities provide additional information on the available offering, and can grant contracting authorities the flexibility necessary to pursue secondary policy objectives when ordering specific products.

Refining product categories would also broaden competition between suppliers at the second stage competition by eliminating product duplication. For example, training materials developed by the US General Services Administration (GSA) to support ordering processes under MAS recommend avoiding the definition of needs according to a specific brand so that competition is not limited.

ChileCompra could further support contracting authorities to increase efficiency with framework agreements

ChileCompra could develop support and guidance to help contracting authorities drive efficiencies through framework agreements. An area of particular importance for additional support is second stage competition. While it represents a minor share of the total number of purchase orders (approximately 0.1% of the total number processed each year), orders passed after second stage competition amount, on average, to slightly more than 28% of total expenditure under framework agreements for the last four years. This represented, in real value, USD 1.84 billion out of the USD 6.5 billion spent in total under framework agreements between 2012 and 2015.

Second stage competition is a strategic milestone in procurement under framework agreements as it represents the achievement of all previous efforts in designing and issuing call for tenders and in selecting the most advantageous proposals. If this step is not adequately carried out, all previous centralised efforts, for example towards sustainable procurement, would be harmed. Second stage competition also represents a more complex step which, in order to drive efficiencies, implies having recourse to strategic procurement skills that go beyond a mere understanding of the operating environment of framework agreements. In Chile, 1 268 calls for second stage competition were made in 2015, compared to a total of 124 665 purchase orders made under framework agreements in 2014. This number raises concerns when considering that the calls had, on average, an 18.8% response rate from suppliers; and that 599 of the calls (47%) had a response rate of less than 10%, and 309 between 10% and 20% (Figure 4.5).

Figure 4.5. Dispersion of suppliers' response rate to calls for second-stage competition, 2015

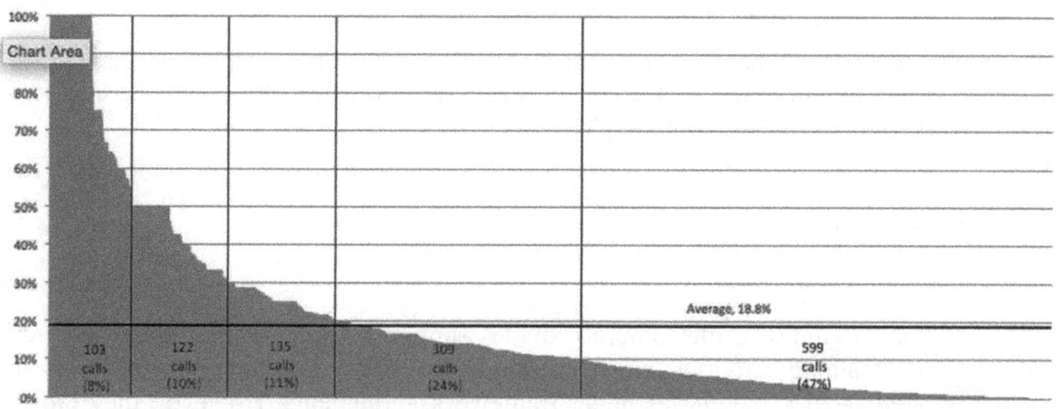

Source: OECD analysis based on information provided by ChileCompra.

ChileCompra Express is used by 850 contracting authorities. On its website, ChileCompra provides guidance to this category of end-users comprised of both mandatory (central government) and voluntary users (municipalities). However, guides could move from the existing operational description of processes to providing further information on how to make the most out of framework agreements. These guides could possibly be tailored to specific audiences.

Box 4.1. Support provided to eligible agencies in New Zealand

The New Zealand Government Procurement (NZGP) agency, under the Ministry of Business, Innovation and Employment, is responsible for the management of collaborative procurement instruments, such as all-of-government (AoG) contracts, which can be used by eligible agencies to purchase a range of products. AoG contracts harness the collective purchasing power of government by establishing single supply agreements for the supply of selected common goods and services.

In addition to AoG contracts led by NZGP, the following two types of collaborative contracts are also available to eligible agencies:

- Open syndicated (OS) contracts
- Common capability (CC) contracts

Dedicated centres of expertise in NGZP manage the development, negotiation, provider performance, and on-going contract management of the AoG contract within New Zealand's government procurement.

Centres of expertise help eligible agencies assess the value that the AoG contract can deliver, both at the implementation phase and throughout the life of the contract. This could include general advice relating to the contract, assistance with analysis of the savings the eligible agency can achieve through the contract, as well as additional value that can be achieved through best practice purchasing.

To further assist eligible agencies in their purchasing operations under AoGs, NGZP has developed quick informative guides specific to each AoG. They provide an overview of:

- key features, benefits and scope of the contract
- the panel of providers
- contractual relationships amongst all parties
- how to join, transition to and buy from this contract

Among the various benefits of the contract, NGZP lists the different procurement options available under the AoG and the direct and indirect specific potential savings that could be generated through this type of procurement.

Source: New Zealand Government Procurement (2016), *All-of-Government Contracts* available at http://www.business.govt.nz/procurement/all-of-government-contracts/current-all-of-government-contracts, consulted on 10 February 2016.

In addition to guides, ChileCompra provides support to contracting authorities via a call centre and training activities, either physically or online. Some training modules are specifically dedicated to purchases under framework agreements. However, they mostly provide an overview of the system, covering how to use the platform and the main milestones to be observed. They do not provide detailed information on the overarching principles of framework agreements, how to understand their structure, or how to increase their efficiencies.

Each framework agreement contains a number of specificities that need to be clearly understood by contracting authorities to allow for informed purchasing decisions. ChileCompra could establish an efficiency checklist for each framework agreement. For example, guidance on the benefits of a procurement planning exercise for office supplies could help contracting authorities to generate further economies of scale by grouping orders. For more complex services, additional information on needs definition or award criteria would support end-users in identifying proposals offering the best value for money overall.

ChileCompra could provide support to contracting authorities in further developing these skills. While taking into account human resources limitations, analyses of contracting authorities' procurement behaviours (recurrence of purchase orders, numbers of second stage competition, most purchased goods and services, etc.) could provide insights into defining the corresponding training strategy.

While training and support in this area would increase the strategic use of framework agreements by contracting authorities, genuine competition among awarded suppliers at the call-off stage could be hindered by publicly disclosed information on the electronic platform. Although transparency is one of the pillars of public procurement at all stages, the timing of the disclosure of some information can impact competition. For the second stage competition, all suppliers invited to submit a bid can clearly see the list of suppliers to whom the invitation was sent, but also those who have submitted a bid before the deadline. This practice could potentially discourage some suppliers from submitting a proposal, and knowing who has already responded risks collusive behaviours among bidders. ChileCompra could reconsider the timing of disclosing information on the identity of suppliers who have reached the second stage competition so that it neither harms genuine competition, nor enables bid-rigging.

ChileCompra could provide information to contracting authorities on the value for money of proposals submitted by bidders to support informed purchasing decisions

Many OECD countries are devoting substantial efforts to channelling procurement spent under framework agreements to suppliers who best meet end-users needs or the adopted procurement strategies. For example, the French centralised purchasing body implemented, in certain framework agreements, a bid rotation system whereby the suppliers best ranked in the initial competition stage are provided with greater revenue certainty. Unless duly justified, contracting authorities are then mandated to order goods and services from the best ranked suppliers.

In accordance with a survey carried out by the Danish Competition Authority on suppliers awarded under a framework agreement, revenue certainty (or uncertainty) is the most decisive factor in a supplier's decision to participate in a call for tender for a framework agreement (Danish Competition and Consumer Authority, 2015).

Figure 4.6. Proportion of non-transacting suppliers and revenue shares of top 10 suppliers in each framework agreement

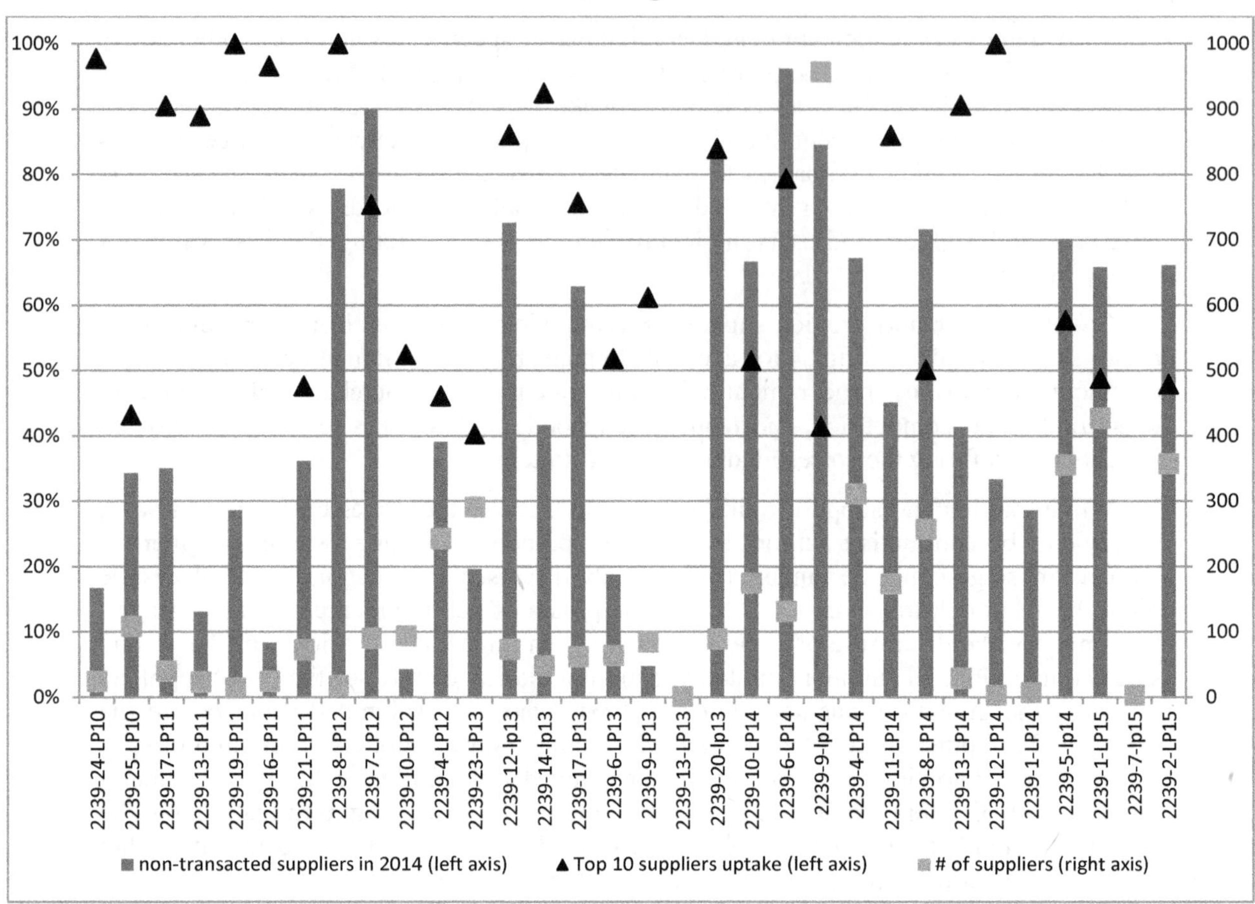

Source: OECD analysis based on information provided by ChileCompra.

Figure 4.6 illustrates that in almost all framework agreements implemented by ChileCompra, a high proportion of awarded suppliers (more than 60%) did not received any purchase orders in 2014. In addition, revenues provided to the first ten suppliers in each framework agreement accounted, on average, for 71% of total procurement expenditure under these procurement instruments.

Although it is important that the inclusiveness of the system is not compromised, ChileCompra could implement measures to incentivise suppliers to submit proposals that maximise value for money, particularly for orders placed below the threshold that do not require a second stage competition. For example, disclosing the initial assessment of suppliers from which the selected good or service could be sourced would provide contracting authorities with additional information on the outcomes of the competition before deciding which supplier to use.

In Finland, Hansel, the central purchasing body of the Finnish government, actively promotes corporate social responsibility in its framework agreements. This objective encompasses various perspectives, such as the environmental performance of goods and services, and financial or social responsibility. Based on a feasibility study, it is decided whether these perspectives can be integrated into the evaluation process. If so, offers submitted by suppliers are assessed against these criteria, which form part of the overall ranking of suppliers. This selection method helps to channel procurement spend to companies, which fits with broader government objectives and strategies.

Ensuring value for money for contracting authorities, notably in second-stage competition, could be achieved by factoring in the outcomes of the initial assessment of the proposals received in purchasing decisions. Part of the initial assessment could serve as a starting point for the second stage competition. By informing suppliers under the framework agreement about initial assessments, companies would compete more fiercely in the first phase, as they know that initial efforts are taken into account. Furthermore, suppliers will also be provided with the opportunity to react and adapt their second proposals, which would result in better overall outcomes for contracting authorities.

References

Albano G. L. and C. Nicholas (2016), *The law and economy of framework agreements: designing flexible solutions for public procurement*, Cambridge University Press.

Danish Competition and Consumer Authority (2015), *Study on competition on public procurement through central framework agreements*, http://en.kfst.dk/~/media/KFST/Publikationer/Engelsk/2015/20150416 COI.pdf.

New Zealand Government Procurement (2016), *All-of-Government Contracts,* http://www.business.govt.nz/procurement/all-of-government-contracts/current-all-of-government-contracts (accessed 10 February 2016).

OECD (2015), *Survey on Centralised Framework Agreements*, OECD, Paris.

OECD (2013), *Public Procurement Review of the Mexican Institute of Social Security: Enhancing Efficiency and Integrity for Better Health Care*, OECD Public Governance Reviews, OECD Publishing, Paris, http://dx.doi.org/10.1787/9789264197480-en.

Chapter 5.

Effective management for a better performance of framework agreements in Chile

Effective framework agreements aim to deliver several benefits to the public sector: they generate economies of scale, avoid duplication and reduce red tape costs. Multidimensional assessment tools should be developed and used to ensure that these collaborative procurement instruments deliver on their initial promises. This chapter examines efforts undertaken by ChileCompra and other countries to monitor the overall performance of framework agreements. It analyses related challenges, notably in obtaining supporting information.

Effective procurement operations only exist when the contractor has been satisfactorily executing its assigned work. However, assessments of the effectiveness of strategic procurement should go beyond ensuring that suppliers deliver what they were asked for, it should also assess the efficiency of procurement in various dimensions.

As a strategic procurement tool, a framework agreement is meant to achieve a number of goals, such as generating economies of scale, limiting duplication and reducing red tape costs for demand and supply sides. The assessment of a framework agreement's efficiencies should therefore examine their performance in all of these dimensions.

Benefits of framework agreements are multidimensional, so should be their assessment

The assessment of procurement performance necessitates developing processes and frameworks to retrieve transactional information. OECD member countries share a strong willingness to identify a set of relevant data that enables the measurement of how procurement operations perform, and the impact of procurement on broader policy objectives. However, in the OECD survey, countries also continuously reported significant challenges in terms of data collection and consistency (OECD, 2013). These impediments also exist for the assessment of how centralised framework agreements perform.

Due to their central role, central purchasing bodies (CPBs) offer a unique opportunity to analyse public procurement efficiencies when using framework agreements. With the increasing use of e-procurement platforms to manage orders under this procurement instrument, CPBs have readily accessible information that allows for the development of meaningful performance indicators adapted to framework agreements.

However, while being an important actor in public procurement, most CPBs lack visibility of the challenges of public procurement under framework agreements, ranging from purchase orders to supplier performance. These elements are important for a comprehensive performance assessment of framework agreements.

In an attempt to address this challenge, some countries, such as Korea, have tried to integrate e-procurement systems with broader public finance management systems, with the aim of providing visibility on the execution phase of purchase orders. Other countries, such as Italy, have put more emphasis on ad-hoc or institutionalised feedback on supplier performance from contracting authorities.

Data consistency is an additional challenge, particularly for performance assessments. Due to the specific operating environment of framework agreements, information is inputted into an electronic procurement system by different stakeholders, which poses the question of how to develop a common typology and agreed vocabulary.

Irrespective of the aspects measured, performance indicators are inherently dependent on data, and countries regularly report challenges in collecting procurement information from decentralised contracting authorities (OECD, 2014). Therefore, a consensus has to be found on the typology of data to be collected and the quality control processes in place to ensure comparability. Further attention should also be placed on definitions of procurement information that is to be collected. This should be widely communicated internally to ensure either the collection of standardised information across sub-national contracting authorities, or the availability of a correlation table.

Centralised framework agreements aggregate needs from different and heterogeneous contracting authorities. Therefore, the first dimension of the framework agreement's efficiency to measure should be its level of adequacy in meeting end-user needs.

The impact of framework agreements on contracting authorities and the recurrence of purchases in a specific product category are among the main reasons cited by OECD countries for implementing a framework agreement. Therefore, the effectiveness of this instrument in achieving this goal constitutes the first step of measuring a framework agreement's performance.

This assessment could be conducted in two ways: the subjective satisfaction of contracting authorities towards a specific framework agreement, and the objective matching of user needs against the offering provided in the instrument. While the first assessment could be subject to the issuance of periodic surveys or debriefing meetings with contracting authorities, the second assessment requires hard evidence from the analyses of transactional data.

The level of subjective satisfaction of contracting authorities is often high, since the general benefits of framework agreements are commonly acknowledged (NAO, 2010). However, strategically using this procurement tool entails purchasing decisions from contracting authorities that should rely on a series of information, from the existence of the framework agreements to the tangible benefits that can be reaped from its use.

Box 5.1. Framework agreements in the United Kingdom

The National Audit Office in the United Kingdom carried out a survey on the use of collaborative procurement across the public sector in eight product categories. To do this, an online questionnaire was sent to 291 heads of procurement across central government bodies, health trusts and local authorities. The questionnaire received a response rate of 64%.

Out of the responses, 93% of the public bodies had used a framework agreement during 2008-09. However, there was a wide variation in the amount of spending that individual bodies were channeling through these existing arrangements.

Among those bodies that had used framework arrangements in 2008-09, 84% of heads of procurement believed that these arrangements had always or often resulted in better value for money than could have been achieved by acting alone. And, 83% thought there was potential to improve value for money by increasing collaboration.

Analysis shows that there were a significant number of heads of procurement who felt the quality of procurement management information available to their body was poor or very poor. Around 5% did not know how to rate the quality of their procurement management information. Although 79% of bodies often compared product specifications to those in existing collaborative arrangements, there was a significant number that did not regularly make comparisons. A quarter of heads of procurement stated that they held poor, very poor or no information on both the overall supply market and their current suppliers' performance.

Although more than half believed that there was sufficient information available about collaborative arrangements across six of the eight categories, a significant number thought that there was not sufficient information, or did not know.

More than half of the bodies did not produce, for any of their significant procurement exercises, key evaluation documents of a business case, supply option analysis or an evaluation of existing collaborative arrangements.

Source: NAO (2010), *A Review of Collaborative Procurement Across Public Sector*, National Audit Office, https://www.nao.org.uk/report/a-review-of-collaborative-procurement-across-the-public-sector-4/ (accessed 19 January 2016).

The level of public procurement expenditure channelled through framework agreements for each specific product category could be a first indication of the extent of response to user needs. Further analyses on procurement expenditure by voluntary users under framework agreements could give additional insights into whether framework agreements are globally appealing.

In addition to the global level of coverage of framework agreements, procurement trends for products available within each instrument could provide central purchasing bodies with a greater understanding of contracting authorities' needs, powerful information that would help to design future procurement strategies. This analysis would also offer linkages with assessments of the performance of framework agreements in generating economies of scale and reducing red tape costs at central and local levels.

Greater aggregation of demand through a limited number of standardised products is understood as having the potential to generate economies of scale (Albano and Nicholas, 2016). However, as previously discussed, economies of scale are likely to be found in products where production costs comprise a sizeable fraction of fixed costs. Should these costs be less prone to variations of production volumes, the greater the aggregation of purchases, the lower the unit cost of each product.

The grouping of purchases has the potential to attract more competitive pricing from suppliers, as well as having a direct impact on processing costs. Analysing the costs deriving of issuing purchase orders would give a basis for calculations of administrative savings for contracting authorities that are generated by the use of the framework agreements. Parameters could encompass various dimensions, such as costs related to the absence of distinct procurement processes, the duration of these avoided steps, and the reduction of the ordering period.

While performance assessments of framework agreements often attempt to measure their impact on red tape costs for contracting authorities, a comprehensive evaluation of performance should also integrate the influence of framework agreements on operational management costs within the CPB. This is particularly true when centralised entities have discretionary decision powers over the implementation, typology and coverage of framework agreements. When the decision to implement or renew framework agreements lies with CPBs, it includes a cost-benefit assessment of its impact on centralised operational management activities.

However, factoring in the centralised administrative costs necessary to implement framework agreements would only provide a partial assessment of the impact of framework agreements on CPBs. There is also the cost of manageing the electronic system where goods and services are available for ordering, and where products are updated. Post-award management activities often account for a significant share of CPB resources, both financial and human.

Time spent on managing awarded framework agreements depends on two major factors: the rules and procedures defined for the management of the product database, and the likely recurrence of request for changes submitted by awarded suppliers. Frameworks that provide guiding principles to suppliers for requesting modifications to their offering generate less flexibility in terms of changes requested by suppliers. However, they tend to reduce the amount of time allotted to this activity.

The number of suppliers awarded under a framework agreement also impacts the resources needed to manage updates of product information in the electronic system, hence the overall performance of framework agreements.

Assessing the impact and tangible benefits of framework agreements on the public demand side should be complemented by assessing its influence on the supply side. Analysing the performance of framework agreements through the prism of the performance of the suppliers in delivering satisfactory goods and services under framework agreements provides CPBs with comprehensive information on its overall functioning.

Several performance indicators could be developed to measure the impact on suppliers, such as the ratio of suppliers being awarded under framework agreements and effectively receiving purchase orders, and the level of adherence to contractual obligations, including delivery times and payment terms. These indicators would provide helpful information to CPBs in guiding future procurement strategies towards the implementation of framework agreements. It will allow centralised entities to assess the appropriateness of the pool of suppliers, its geographical allocation and the relevance of evaluation criteria to identify committed suppliers.

In countries where suppliers awarded under framework agreements are not obliged to respond to subsequent purchase orders, the ratio of response could provide CPBs with an additional indication of how contracting authorities' needs and market capabilities are matched.

Reducing red tape costs and generating savings

Measuring the performance of framework agreements in OECD countries principally aims to support the initial assessment of the cost benefits ratio that presides over the decision to implement or renew such an instrument.

Management activities under framework agreements impact CPBs as well as the suppliers awarded.

Figure 5.1. Modifications to the offerings allowed for suppliers

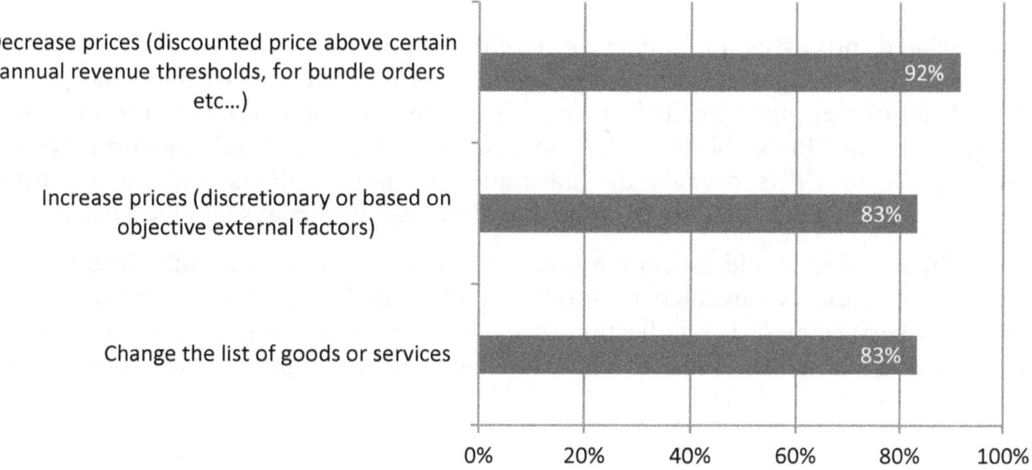

Note: Chile responded yes to allow all three modifications listed in the figure.

Source: OECD (2015), *Survey on Centralised Framework Agreements*, OECD Paris.

Almost all respondents to the OECD survey accept decreased prices proposed by suppliers, which is not surprising considering the overarching philosophy of collaborative procurement instruments. In some instances, bidders have provided initial price submissions without any revenue certainty. Therefore, when there is an aggregation of purchases in purchase orders, suppliers are incentivised to offer discounts. In most of the countries surveyed, CPBs accept other modifications to initial submissions, whether it is a price increase or a change in the offering. These modifications could be useful to keep goods and services provided under framework agreements in line with major market trends and products obsolescence. However, most of the respondents provide a structured framework for these modifications.

Figure 5.2. Framework for modifications of offerings

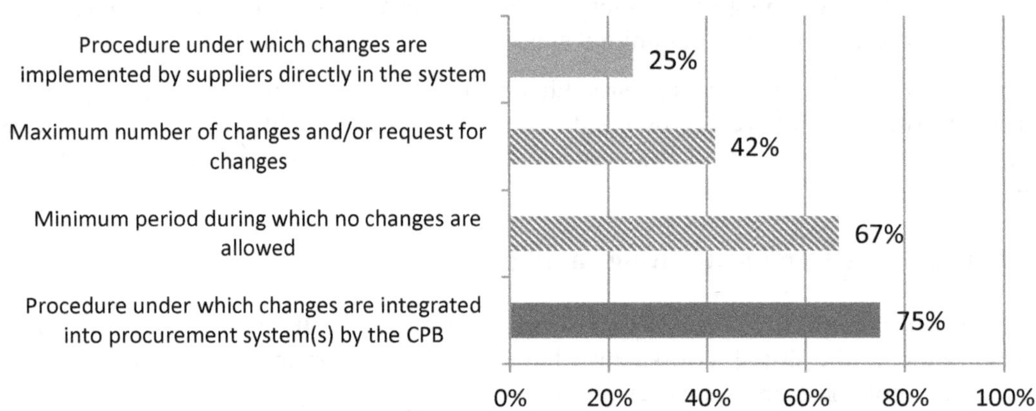

Note: Lighter blue colour indicates where Chile does not take part. Bars with diagonal filling indicate where it is only applicable to some framework agreements in Chile.

Source: OECD (2015), *Survey on Centralised Framework Agreements*, OECD, Paris.

Structured processes to update or modify suppliers' offerings, as part of the framework agreement's operating environment, contribute to framing the overall performance of the agreement. This impacts the competitiveness of the offerings provided by suppliers, and CPB's efforts on the administration of the electronic platform. While a vast majority of CPBs oversee the integration of modifications into the electronic platform, few countries allow suppliers to directly integrate changes into the system.

OECD countries could assess the effectiveness of processes that may lead to well-performing framework agreements, as well as evaluating their objective performance in a number of perspectives. The collection of evidence of how framework agreements are performing could serve various objectives, including shaping future procurement decisions.

Figure 5.3. Information used to monitor framework agreements

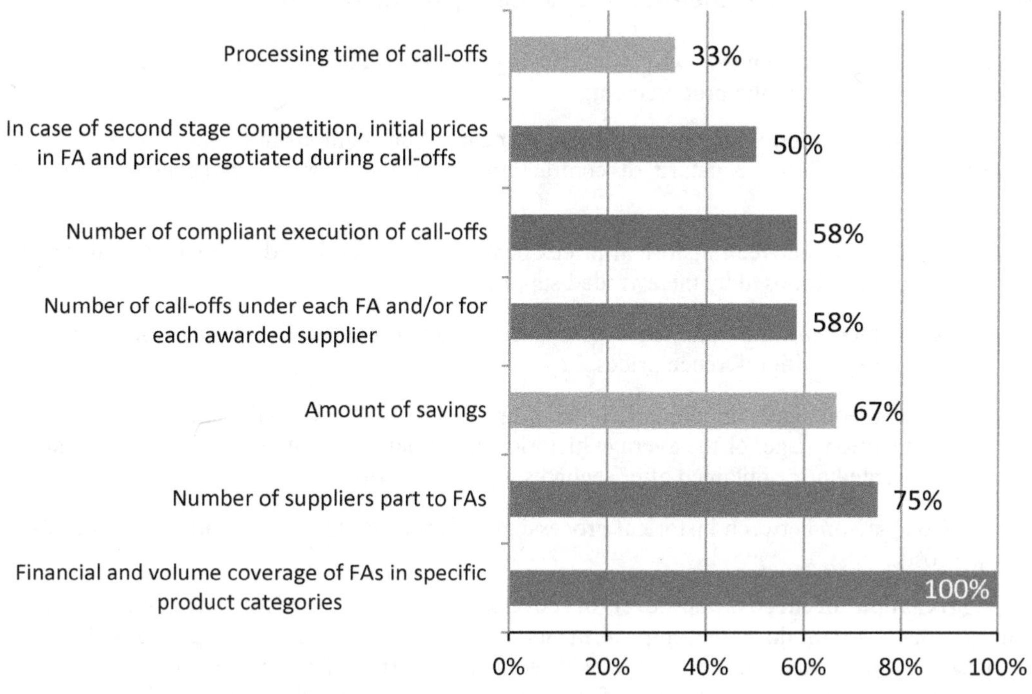

Note: Lighter blue colour indicates where Chile does not take part. FA = framework agreement.

Source: OECD (2015), *Survey on Centralised Framework Agreements*, OECD, Paris.

Framework agreements are designed to yield a number of benefits, such as aggregating needs that generate economies of scale, reducing red tape costs and streamlining processes. It is therefore unsurprising that all respondents evaluate the coverage of framework agreements against a specific product category. The higher the coverage, the greater potential for generating savings from a consolidation of demand.

Although the methods of calculating savings differ across countries, the efficiency of framework agreements in generating financial benefits is assessed by the majority of respondents to the OECD survey. Evaluating the financial performance of frameworks could be realised from two different perspectives: exogenous or endogenous.

Exogenous performance is measured against either prices paid outside the framework agreement or historical prices. In France, savings relating to renewed framework agreements are calculated against historical prices. In Italy, savings are calculated by comparing the awarded value with the average cost paid by the contracting authorities. In Chile, financial savings are calculated on the basis of the difference of the price proposed by bidders awarded under framework agreements, and the average price proposed by at least three suppliers outside the procurement instrument. While this gives initial indications about the competitiveness of framework agreements compared to ad-hoc purchases, the sample size could pose questions on possible selection bias.

Endogenous performance involves evaluating the financial benefits achieved within framework agreements. Where a second stage competition exists, many countries calculate savings using the difference between the initial listed prices and those offered by suppliers after the mini competition.

Box 5.2. Challenges in evaluating the savings generated by framework agreements

The following challenges exist when trying to undertake a comparative evaluation of savings achieved with public procurement:

Calculation methodology: a broad range of calculation methods are applied across OECD countries depending on the nature of contracting mechanisms or the perspective identified, notably:

- Comparison between historical prices or reference price based on market analysis and final price proposed by the awarded supplier.
- Assessment of the total cost of ownership of products or services procured, and comparison with reference prices.
- Comparison between the price list proposed by the awarded suppliers in the first competition stage, or the average historical price paid by contracting authorities, and the discounted price obtained after second stage competition.
- Comparison between historical processing or labour costs and new processing or labour costs.

Aggregation of needs: the level of coverage of CPBs varies greatly among OECD countries, and so to does the impact of its efforts in generating savings throughout the procurement cycle. Accounting for these differences in terms of the involvement of CPBs in carrying out public procurement is vital for ensuring a sound comparison of activities.

Selection bias: defining a common scope of analysis could support meaningful comparison. Information gathered on CPBs in OECD countries shows horizontal or vertical differences in terms of mandates.

Sources:
OECD (2014), *Survey on Public Procurement*, OECD, Paris and OECD (2015), *Survey on Centralised Framework Agreements*, OECD, Paris.

In addition to measuring the financial impact of framework agreements, one third of respondents also assess processing costs compared to ad-hoc procurement cost. Again, different methodologies exist. Chile calculates the savings by estimating the difference between costs related to the issuance of a purchase order under a framework agreement, and the costs generated by the issuance of a public tender or direct award procedure.

While the outcome of this exercise should provide CPBs with tangible information about the level of reduction of red tape costs, and therefore the processual efficiency of framework agreements, this methodology presupposes access to a range of information, which is reportedly not readily available in OECD countries. Assessing this performance perspective implies having information about direct procurement process costs (i.e. procurement officials salaries and standardised timeframes by type of procurement procedures), as well as a harmonised mapping exercise of roles and responsibilities within contracting authorities to ensure that indirect costs, such as hierarchical approvals or budgetary validations, are also taken into account.

Portugal measures processing costs by assessing the administrative impact of the aggregation of demands. Under the Portuguese framework agreement system, contracting authorities can group their orders into one single call-off. Although processual information is needed to attach a financial estimate to this calculation, the initial exercise could provide a relative indication in terms of the percentage of processual costs saved through the use of framework agreements.

Human resource needs for assessing the performance of framework agreements

The implementation of a framework agreement will provide insufficient benefits if not coupled with strategies that aim to further ease the management of the agreement, incentivise the supply side to participate, and provide exhaustive procurement information that allows for the development of meaningful key performance indicators.

ChileCompra could streamline product updates to seize tangible benefits from framework agreements

Streamlining and rationalising the processes related to product updates in ChileCompra Express could be a powerful tool for augmenting the benefits of framework agreements. This will free up ChileCompra's internal resources and allow for a more strategic focus on product category management, resulting in more tailored framework agreements and providing the potential for the development of further instruments.

As of the end of 2015, ChileCompra Express had more than 115 000 different products provided by around 6 000 suppliers. These suppliers can request modifications to their offerings at any point during the term of the framework agreement. They can either request a change in the product specifications and pricing, or add new products. In 2015, ChileCompra received about 436 000 requests for product updates, while almost half (49.3%) of the products under framework agreements were not ordered once. More than 250 000 requests were related to offers at a discounted price for a limited amount of time (Figure 5.4).

The number of requests has a dramatic impact on the human resources dedicated to the operational management of framework agreements, and can hinder the possibility of shifting towards more strategic procurement activities. It is estimated that in 2015, a total of 16 564 hours were spent in processing 436 000 requests, and 46.5 hours were spent, on average per day, in processing requests for new products[1] (Figure 5.4). This work was mostly carried out by category managers, and required almost 10 full-time officials to process, on average, 22 requests per hour. This work almost prevents these procurement officials from concentrating on the market and demand analysis that would allow for strategic decisions on the development of framework agreements. It also leads to challenges for the creation of new framework agreements in other strategic areas that could provide potential for economies of scale through the aggregation of needs, such as in telecommunications, as it will automatically generate an unsustainable increase in operational management time.

Figure 5.4. Number of modification requests and estimated hours spent processing requests per day (2015)

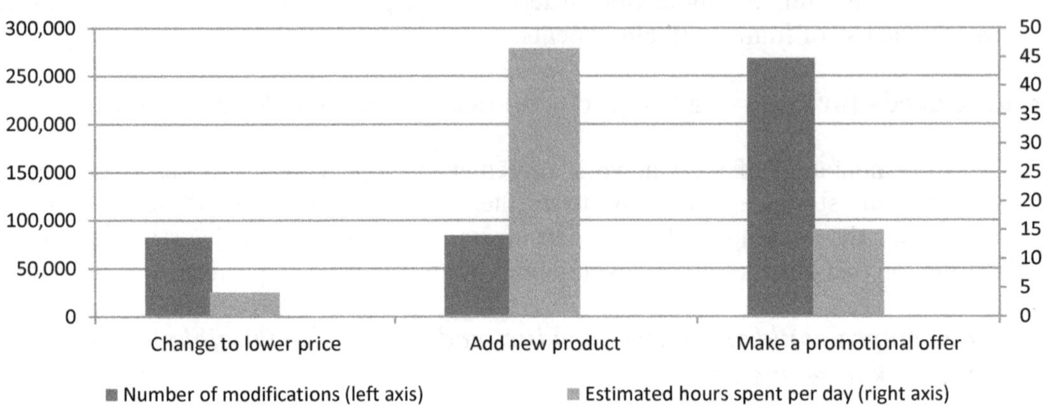

Source: OECD analysis based on information provided by ChileCompra.

ChileCompra should identify alternative means to help address these burdens. As a first step, it could consider revisiting how product modifications are requested by suppliers and validated by ChileCompra.

Processes defined for product updates are structured around the parallel assessment of requests: first from a technical perspective to ensure that technical specifications of changes can be seamlessly integrated into the platform, and second that the change is appropriate from a procurement perspective. These two processes are carried out simultaneously by the respective teams in ChileCompra, which could lead to a duplication of efforts. If the official responsible for assessing the appropriateness of the request concerning the typology of products refuses the modification, the team responsible for ensuring technical compliance will have had worked for nothing. Implementing a sequenced assessment of requests would mitigate the risk of duplicating effort.

Considering the number of requests related to discounted offers, and the relatively straightforward process required to implement these temporary changes, ChileCompra could consider removing the verification step in these cases. This decision would help to reduce the overall workload of teams responsible for product updates by nearly 25%.

Identifying technical solutions to ease product updates processes would provide ChileCompra with immediate tangible benefits.

Box 5.3. Integrating product catalogues and updates in GSA Advantage!

The US General Services Administration (GSA) selects suppliers under the Multiple Award Schedules (MAS) programme. GSA Advantage! is the online platform shopping site for government agencies and contains GSA approved products and services. Using this menu-driven database system, government buyers can search for the products they need, compare prices and product information (in cases where there is more than one supplier), and place their orders.

All GSA schedule contractors are required to submit electronic catalogues and price lists to GSA Advantage! no later than six months after the contract is awarded. They can be submitted using the Schedule Input Program (SIP) software, available for download at the GSA Vendor Support Center (VSC) web site at http://vsc.fss.gsa.gov, or by using the Electronic Data Interchange (EDI) format.

Via those two distinct technologies, contractors under MAS are able to prepare their entire electronic catalogue in a format that will be directly integrated into GSA Advantage! GSA uniquely identifies each product using a combination of the contractor's contract number plus the manufacturer part number. Each product submitted must have a unique manufacturer part number – even if two or more manufacturers carry the exact same part number.

Once the catalogue is uploaded it will be forwarded to the appropriate GSA contracting officer (CO) for review. Once the CO has reviewed the catalog, an email (or fax, phone call) is sent to the contractor stating whether the file was approved or rejected and the reasons for rejection, if applicable. A SIP response file will also be generated after the CO has reviewed the contractor's file.

Files containing temporary price reductions will be immediately loaded onto GSA Advantage! without contracting officer approval.

Source: Adapted from GSA (2015), Vendor Support Centre accessible at https://vsc.gsa.gov/faq/startup-kit.cfm.

ChileCompra could use enhanced technological tools to support and ease the processes related to product updates. To this end, a dedicated Supplier Advisory Board could be created to work on technological transformations to ensure that both ChileCompra's operational constraints and suppliers' technical capabilities are taken into account. This effort would contribute to safeguarding the overall inclusiveness of the system, while providing a more sustainable operating environment for products updates. Technological and processual answers to this challenge will decrease processing costs and burdens within ChileCompra, and unlock the potential to increase the global coverage of framework agreements by providing the opportunity to develop additional instruments.

ChileCompra could develop structured supplier performance assessments to promote the effectiveness of framework agreements

The performance of framework agreements should be assessed from both the supply and demand perspective. Considering the specific relationship implied by this procurement instrument, where suppliers are asked to abide by future and hypothetical requests, a performing environment should ensure that awarded suppliers are fit for purpose.

The satisfactory delivery of goods and services is central for helping contracting authorities to identify suppliers from whom products will be ordered. This component is crucial to the overall effectiveness of framework agreements (Racca, 2010). One of the main duties of CPBs, therefore, is to design and implement contractual relationships with suppliers that are conducive to supplier performance.

Considering the existing limitations of ChileCompra Express, which does not seamlessly integrate information on the execution of orders, supplier performance assessments should be carried out using the electronic system. The source of information relating to order execution resides in the voluntary information provided by contracting authorities. When a purchase order has not been satisfactorily executed, contracting authorities can indicate to ChileCompra that sanctions were applied, and provide the underlying reasons.

This mostly takes the form of contractual penalties corresponding to a share of the total value of the contract. In this respect, a strong, yet proportionate, penalties system helps to ensure that providers will abide by their commitments. The system should be consistently applied across contracting authorities.

In addition to an assessment of supplier performance through sanctions, ChileCompra could develop an inspection process whereby the performance of selected suppliers is thoroughly and independently assessed against specific objectives.

This form of assessment, while not covering the entire pool of suppliers, could provide ChileCompra with detailed evidence about suppliers' commitment to the execution of purchase orders under framework agreements. This type of analysis would also offer ChileCompra the flexibility to focus on issues of particular importance. Depending on strategic orientations, ChileCompra could apply this scheme to vendors in a specific product category, or to high volume vendors across product categories.

Box 5.4. Performance assessment of suppliers in Consip

Consip, the Italian central purchasing body, assesses the performance of its suppliers according to a structured mechanism.

1. Technicalities

The monitoring of service qualitative levels delivered by suppliers is based on the analysis of five macro-categories (for each framework agreement):

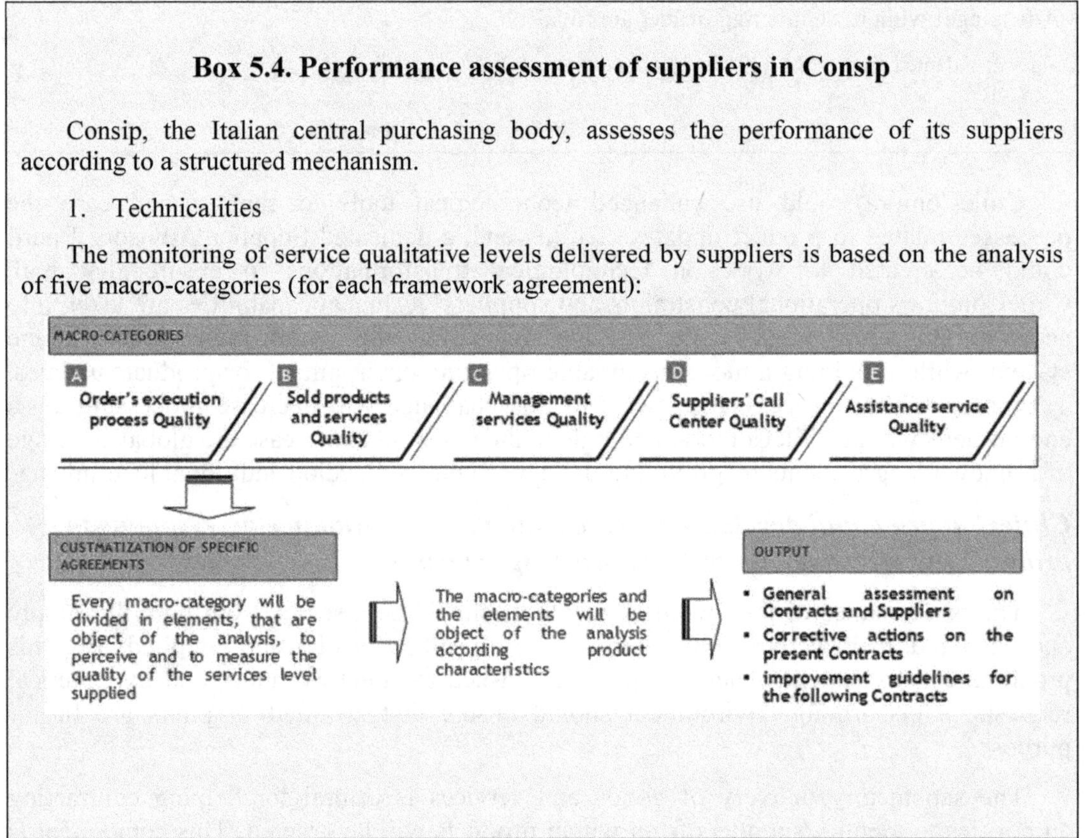

Box 5.4. Performance assessment of suppliers in Consip *(continued)*

2. Tools

The Supplies' Monitoring Team employs the following three tools:

- Inspections: supplier performance inspections aim to verify the meeting of service levels required in the contract agreement (technical requirements). An external inspection body is accredited every two years to develop this activity. Monitored suppliers pay inspection costs.
- Survey: the surveys are finalised to measure the perception of the suppliers' service levels. This activity is developed by an external call centre.
- Claims: collection and analysis of public administration claims is undertaken in order to identify agreements performing below requirements in terms of supplied quality services.

3. Inspection financing

Each agreement generates a specific budget to finance the inspections. This budget is calculated proportionally to the amount of money spent through the agreement (the maximum amount paid by the supplier is equal to 0.5% of the sum spent). Consip authorises the supplier to pay the external inspection body. To guarantee the inspections payments, Consip requires a specific guarantee from the supplier.

4. Methodology

The results of surveys and inspections are used according to different weights to produce an indicator that shows the performance of suppliers under existing framework agreements.

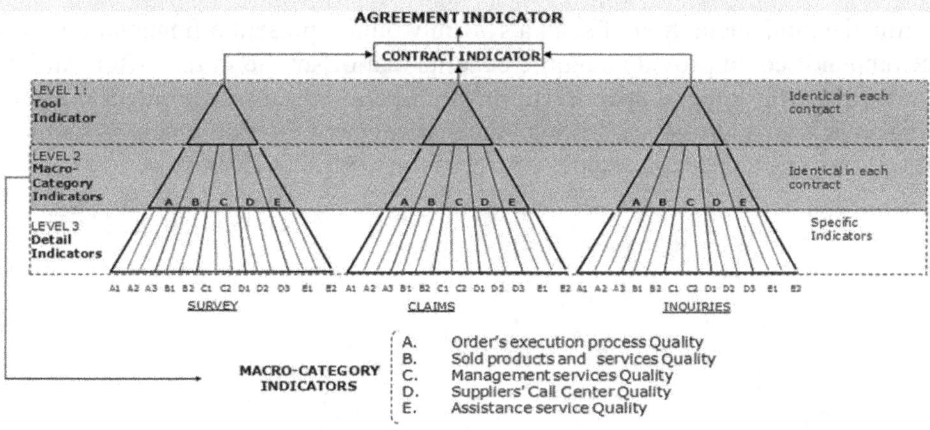

The monitoring team draws on survey and inspection findings to score each component in the indicator. Final assessment is as follows:

Scores	1	2	3	4	5
Level of service % indicator	0%	25%	50%	75%	100%
Range	Alert		Warning		On target

- **Alert** when the score is equal or smaller than 50%
- **Warning** when the score is between 51% and 74%
- **On target** when the score is equal or bigger than 75%

Source: Adapted from OECD (2016), Improving ISSSTE's Public Procurement for Better Results, OECD Publishing Paris

In implementing a structured qualitative assessment of supplier performance that takes into account existing technological limitations, ChileCompra will create room for improved efficiency in the management of framework agreements. By further communicating about these efforts, ChileCompra could strengthen commitment from the supplier community, thereby minimising the application of contractual sanctions and fostering supplier relationship management. This will represent a shift from contract compliance towards contract management.

In implementing a structured qualitative assessment of supplier performance that takes into account existing technological limitations, ChileCompra will create room for improved efficiency in the management of framework agreements. By further communicating about these efforts, ChileCompra could strengthen commitment from the supplier community, thereby minimising the application of contractual sanctions and fostering supplier relationship management. This will represent a shift from contract compliance towards contract management.

Integrated procure-to-pay system would provide ChileCompra with a greater visibility of the overall procurement cycle

The various efforts undertaken by ChileCompra in managing framework agreements would be greatly simplified by the implementation of an electronic platform covering the entire procurement cycle. This will provide the central authority with information relating to the execution of purchase orders, therefore providing readily accessible insights of effective procurement operations under framework agreements.

While the implementation of such a system would represent a financial investment for ChileCompra, it could provide tangible benefits that offset the initial costs. An integrated system would offer integral spend visibility and harmonised procurement information. It would also help to address one of the main challenges of e-procurement systems reported by OECD countries: data consistency and reliability (OECD, 2014).

Box 5.5. Data connections in KONEPS (Korea Online E-Procurement System)

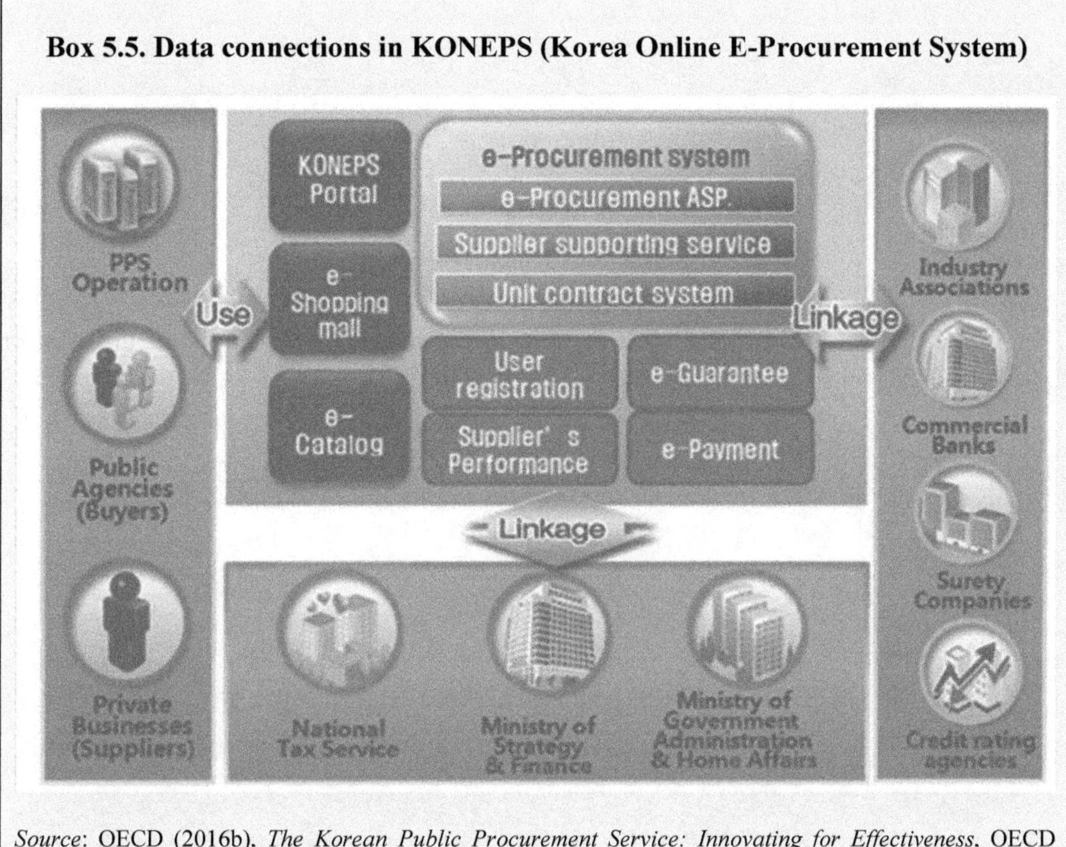

Source: OECD (2016b), *The Korean Public Procurement Service: Innovating for Effectiveness*, OECD Public Governance Reviews, OECD Publishing, Paris, http://dx.doi.org/10.1787/9789264249431-en.

Integrated procure-to-pay systems provide ChileCompra with greater visibility on the entire procurement cycle under framework agreements, from historical spending to the execution of purchases orders. In addition, they can also minimise suppliers' participation costs, since the administrative documents and certifications necessary for participation in public procurement are retrieved directly from the electronic systems of other public or private institutions.

In Korea, 477 document forms have been converted into digital equivalents. A 2009 study conducted by Hanyang University indicated that these changes led to an estimated USD 8 billion in annual transaction-cost savings – primarily for the private sector in reduced costs for visiting public entities, obtaining required certificates and proof documents, and registering and updating accounts in multiple systems.

Note

1 Based on the estimated total hours spent in 2015 provided by ChileCompra, this number was calculated on the assumption of 21 working days per month, on average.

References

Albano G. L., Nicholas C. (2016), *The law and economy of framework agreements: designing flexible solutions for public procurement*, Cambridge University Press.

GSA (2015), Vendor Support Centre, https://vsc.gsa.gov/faq/startup-kit.cfm.

NAO (2010), *A Review of Collaborative Procurement Across the Public Sector*, National Audit Office, UK.

OECD (2016a), Improving ISSSTE's Public Procurement for Better Results, OECD Publishing Paris, http://dx.doi.org/10.1787/9789264249899-en.

OECD (2016b), *The Korean Public Procurement Service: Innovating for Effectiveness*, OECD Public Governance Reviews, OECD Publishing, Paris, http://dx.doi.org/10.1787/9789264249431-en.

OECD (2015), *Survey on Centralised Framework Agreements*, OECD, Paris.

OECD (2014), *Survey on Public Procurement*, OECD, Paris.

OECD (2013), *Implementing the OECD Principles for Integrity in Public Procurement: Progress since 2008*, OECD Publishing, Paris, http://dx.doi.org/10.1787/9789264201385-en.

Racca (2010), "Collaborative Procurement and Contract Performance in the Italian Healthcare Sector: Illustration of a Common Problem in European Procurement", *Public Procurement Law Review*, No. 3, 2010, http://ssrn.com/abstract=1714278.

Chapter 6.

An action plan to develop the way forward

This chapter makes recommendations for ChileCompra to revisit the design and management of its framework agreements. By comparing the benefits obtained in various OECD countries, it suggests policy options that ChileCompra could consider to further strengthen the strategic approach to its centralised procurement function. Policy options are structured against the procurement cycle following a phased approach, this allows for immediate additional efficiencies and for more long-term transformational changes.

Considering the current use of this procurement instrument, and its success in terms of inclusiveness, the sound implementation of recommendations towards a more efficient system would require a cautious and phased approach to avoid drastic and unprepared changes.

Table 6.1. Phased recommendations to revisit framework agreements in Chile

<table>
<tr><th rowspan="2">Phase of framework agreement</th><th colspan="2">Recommendations</th></tr>
<tr><th>Short term</th><th>Long term</th></tr>
<tr><td>Preparing</td><td>ChileCompra could:
• Develop regional lots, taking into consideration the heterogeneity of the market structure and the contracting authority's needs, and not necessarily the administrative division of the country.
• Tailor the duration of framework agreements according to its costs and benefits.
• Examine and review the demand analysis and procurement strategy on framework agreements with a low coverage of public expenditure.</td><td>ChileCompra could:
• Differentiate the instruments and their implementation and strategies, for instance, implement a dynamic purchasing system for products/ services where fulfilling technical requirements is deemed sufficient for identifying suitable suppliers.
• Develop further demand analysis on the market concentration and sector-specific characteristics of all framework agreements that could be enhanced through the integration of ChileCompra with a public finance management system.</td></tr>
<tr><td>Tendering and awarding</td><td>ChileCompra could:
• Engage with suppliers from the early stage by:
– Regularly publishing procurement plans on ChileCompra's website, or on a platform for national procurement, to inform all stakeholders on upcoming opportunities,
– Publishing prior information notices with sufficient information to give visibility to economic operators.
– Further utilising all components of requests for information before the publication of a framework work agreement.
– Institutionalising meetings with suppliers before launching of a framework agreement.
• Work closely with other institutions, such as industry associations and Chambers of Commerce.
• Allow for the allotment, subcontracting and grouping of small and medium-sized enterprises.
• Engage with contracting authorities from the early stage.</td><td>ChileCompra could:
• Further tailor the procurement process depending on the sector and the complexity of the framework agreement. In particular, early engagement with suppliers could expedite the process.
• Further develop subject matter expertise of the public procurement workforce.
• Standardise categories and subcategories of goods and services.
• Reduce the number of suppliers, depending on the nature of the framework agreement.
• Introduce a prequalification stage with additional capability tests; include past performance of suppliers as a criterion.</td></tr>
<tr><td>Launching</td><td>ChileCompra could:
• Streamline the ordering process and eliminate unnecessary levels of details when describing needs.
• Provide support and guidance to contracting authorities in second-stage competition based on their procurement behaviour.
• Develop and make available an efficiency checklist tailored for each framework agreement to allow contracting authorities to make informed purchasing decisions.</td><td>ChileCompra could:
• Revisit product categorisation to ensure an adequate level of competition.
• Provide support to contracting authorities through a call centre and training activities, either physically or online. Cover operational aspects as well as the overarching principles of framework agreements.
• Implement measures aimed at promoting suppliers who provide the best value for money. This could include disclosure of the initial assessment of suppliers, the bid rotation system, etc.</td></tr>
</table>

Table 6.1. Phased recommendations to revisit framework agreements in Chile *(continued)*

Phase of framework agreement	Recommendations	
	Short term	Long term
Managing	ChileCompra could: • Revisit and identify appropriate technical solutions for the product modification request process for suppliers and ChileCompra. • Carry out supplier performance assessments on the electronic platform. • Ensure the consistent application of penalties across contracting authorities. • Communicate on efforts made towards a structure for the qualitative assessment of supplier performance.	ChileCompra could: • Streamline and rationalise the product update process in ChileCompra Express. • Establish a Supplier Advisory Board dedicated to technological transformation to enhance such tools and ease product update processes. • Develop an inspection process whereby the performance of selected suppliers is thoroughly and independently assessed against specific objectives. • Implement an electronic platform covering the entire procurement cycle.

The above recommendations are focusing on three different streams of actions, all of which applicable across the entire procurement cycle. ChileCompra could invest in efforts towards the streamlining of existing processes, the improvement of their effectiveness or further increase the efficiency of the system.

Figure 6.1. Recommendations on the implementation of revised framework agreements

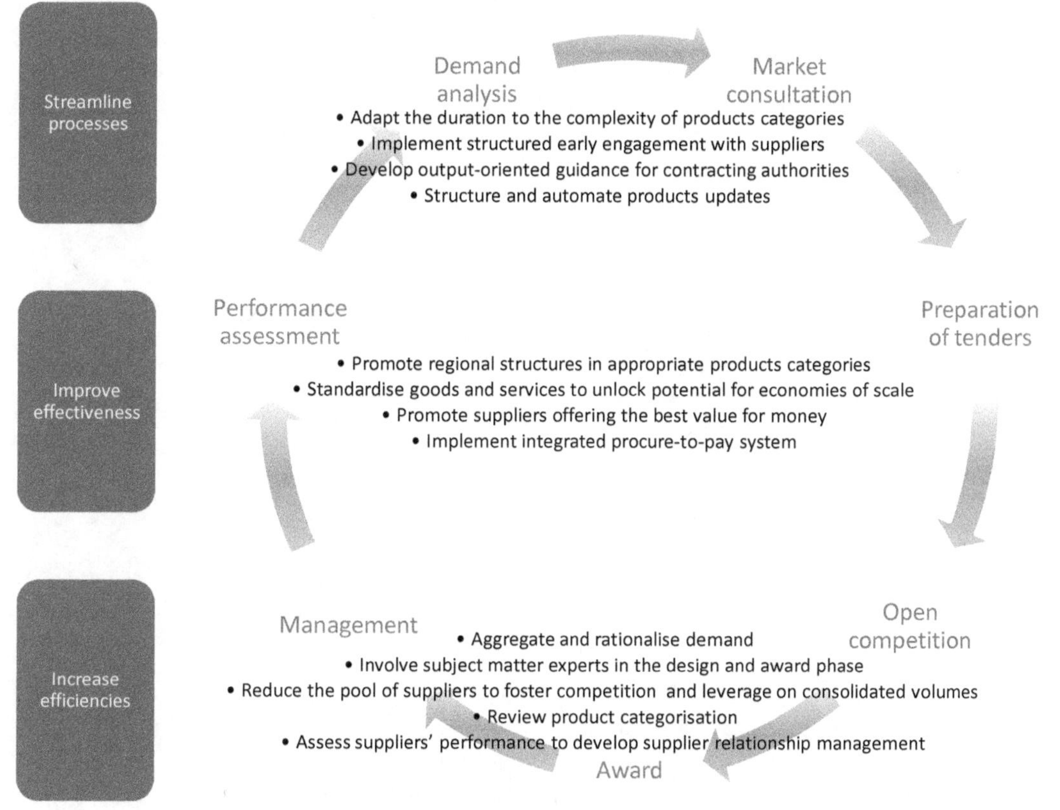

Source: Produced by the OECD Secretariat.

Annex A.

Australia: Raising supplier awareness of tendering processes

Background

To meet business needs, Western Australian government public authorities look for value for money contracting solutions. More than 40 000 individual contracts are established each year between public authorities and private sector suppliers. These contracts supply a diverse range of Western Australian government business needs, from the purchasing of information technology to the engagement of consultants.

To win a contract through a Western Australian Government public authority, bidders should satisfy some requirements that evaluate their ability to fulfil the request's requirements. The contracting authority will determine the number of suppliers under the framework agreement. To make sure that suppliers understand the requirements, the department of finance of the Western Australia government published online the "Suppliers Guide to Tendering – Products and Services".

Implementation

The guide provides information on the Western Australian government's tendering processes. It helps the bidder to prepare and submit offers, and supports them to provide products and services to government.

The guide also gives very clear guidance on requirements and selection criteria. The first two requirements are assessed on a yes/no basis:

- Pre-qualification requirements:

Each requirement will be assessed on a yes/no basis. They are not given a numeric score. Bidders must answer all requirements if they want their response to be considered. An assessment of "no" against any requirement will eliminate the bidder from further consideration.

- Compliance and disclosure requirements:

Each requirement will be assessed on a yes/no basis. They are not given a numeric score. Bidders must answer all of these requirements if they want their response to be considered. If a compliance requirement is not met, it may eliminate the bidder response from consideration

This is an efficient way to automatically eliminate bidders not fulfilling requirements as public officials do not have to conduct a deep analysis of the qualification criteria and can thus concentrate on the valid tenders.

- Qualitative requirements:

Qualitative requirements are used by the Evaluation Panel to identify the requirements of the request and evaluate the ability of the bidder to successfully perform these requirements. As a general rule, they will include such things as:

- Product requests (suitability of proposed products, ability to meet project timeframes, service and maintenance, demonstrated experience in completing similar projects, and "buy local").
- Service requests (a demonstrated understanding of the required tasks, skills and expertise of the key personnel relevant to this requirement, demonstrated experience in completing similar projects, project timeframes, "buy local").

Qualitative requirements are normally weighted. It is therefore important to give significant consideration to requirements with a higher weighting. This will have a significant influence on the selection process.

The framework agreement will be awarded to suppliers depending on their ranking and the rules set out in the tender specifications.

- Price

Price is the dollar value of the response. This is based on the predetermined pricing schedule outlined in the request. It is very important that the bidder completes the pricing in exactly the format asked for in the request. The bidder must also be prepared to maintain the price for a period of time known as the "validity period", which will be specified in the request.

- Value for money

When a supplier addresses the selection requirements, it is important to demonstrate how their submission represents value for money for the Western Australian government.

Key lessons learned

A guide for suppliers is a good way to make them aware of tendering processes in the public sector. This document can be used as a reference to understand the tendering process.

The assessment of questions on a yes/no basis, with the elimination of suppliers with "no" answers, enables the bids to be analysed efficiently.

For further information visit: www.finance.wa.gov.au/cms/uploadedFiles/Government_Procurement/Guidelines_and_templates/goods_and_services_suppliers_guide_to_tendering.pdf.

Annex B.

Finland: Template of feasibility studies for the implementation of framework agreements

Hansel, the central government purchasing body in Finland, developed structured feasibility studies to decide on the implementation of framework agreements. The outline below details the elements which are considered to assess the feasibility of using such procurement instrument.

- Section 1: Background and benefits:
  - Summary and background of the framework agreement
  - Savings to the state budget
  - Financial benefits of the framework agreement for the central purchasing body (CPB) if fees are to be received
  - Other benefits of the framework to the CPB
  - Effect on other framework agreements
  - Benefits to contracting authorities
- Section 2: Analysis of the current framework agreement or the overall situation
  - General
  - Volume, vendors and contracting authorities
  - Contracting authority feedback
  - Feedback from the vendors and the market place
  - Functionality of current call-off system
  - Functionality of terms and conditions
  - Summary of the current framework agreement
- Section 3: Market analysis
  - Market size and the state's procurement volume in relation to market size
  - Market structure
  - Most important vendors in the market
  - Uniformity and maturity of the market
  - Market development outlook for the next four years

- Section 4: Contracting authorities' analysis
  - Current and upcoming needs of the contracting authorities
  - Most important contracting authorities, volumes and current agreements
  - Contracting authorities' reference group
- Section 5: Stakeholder analysis and steering of procurement at the state administration
  - Stakeholder analysis
  - Steering of procurement at the state administration
- Section 6: Framework agreement design strategy
  - Scope of the procurement (minimum, maximum, alternative procurement methods, limits)
  - Duration of the framework agreement
  - Call-off model for the framework agreement
  - Contracting authorities' call-off support
  - Contracting authorities' duties and liabilities in relation to the vendor
  - Impact on secondary policy objectives (small and medium-sized enterprises, green, innovation, etc)
  - Usage of e-Systems
  - Qualifying criteria
  - Price
  - Quality
- Section 7: Tendering process
  - CPB's expertise in relation to the industry
  - How challenging and large the tendering process is
  - Resources fixed from the procurement sector for the tendering process
  - Usage of external resources during the tendering process
  - Summary of the tendering process
- Section 8: Vendor management
  - CPB's tasks during the contracting period
  - CBP's resources for vendor management
  - Alternative solutions if framework agreement is unavailable

Annex C.

France: Volume consolidation and number of awarded suppliers[1]

Background

- The Union of Public Purchasing Groups (UGAP, *Union des groupements d'achats publics*) is a central purchasing body (CPB) that buys products and services under the French Public Procurement Code (*Code des marchés publics*), which is based on European Union (EU) public procurement Directive 2014/24/EU. UGAP then sells these products and services to the government and government agencies, local and regional authorities, and hospitals. Its purchasing categories include vehicles, IT, furniture and equipment, medical supplies, maintenance and technical services, and facility management services.
- One of the main goals of the CPB is to secure procurement, avoiding any supply disruption and boosting competition to achieve better value for money. The CPB has to consider specific rules available under the public procurement code for each product/service category to achieve its goals.
- Paper is a very strategic procurement category as it is the first consumable used by contracting authorities. The market structure is oligopolistic (only a few manufacturers in the world and around 10 suppliers) and became more and more competitive with the demand decrease. The demand decrease in France is due to several reasons, such as the generalisation of dematerialisation and policies to decrease the consumption of paper.
- The framework agreement on paper has become even more strategic since the state imposed its mandatory use by all entities of central government. This is why the CPB has to find a system to help more than one supplier receive orders.

Implementation and process

The strategy adopted for this framework agreement was based on the rotation system, where more than one supplier receives a share of the contract. The framework agreement has two lots, one on eco-responsible paper delivered with handling, and the other without handling.

The general rules are set in the tender specifications as follows:

- Up to six suppliers under the framework agreement.
- The framework agreement is concluded for a maximum of three years (two years with a possibility to extend it twice for six months).

- Each contract issued from the mini-tender will be concluded for a maximum of 12 months.
- The estimated amount of the framework agreement is around EUR 80 million.
- The award criteria for the framework agreement are based on environmental aspects, quality of service, and technical value. They are not based on price. The price criterion will be used for mini-tenders.
- For each mini-tender, the CPB has to determine the minimum and maximum amount of the contract.
- Up to three suppliers under the contract resulting from the mini-tender:
  - The supplier ranked first will get 70% of the minimum amount
  - The supplier ranked second will get 30% of the minimum amount

If the amount ordered is over the minimum amount:

- The supplier ranked first will get 70% of the maximum amount
- The supplier ranked second will get 30% of the maximum amount

In case of failure of the supplier ranked first in the mini-tender, the orders will go to the second supplier. In case of failure of the supplier ranked second in the mini-tender, the orders will go to the first. In case of failure of suppliers ranked first and second in the mini-tender, the orders will go to the supplier ranked third.

This distribution of the volume of the contract will lead to a high competition, since suppliers are encouraged to be ranked first. This is one of the reasons why the supplier ranked third does not receive any order (as well as to avoid any risk of collusion).

Key lessons learned

The framework agreement was concluded with the main four paper suppliers representing more than 50% of the market share. This new system enabled a significant increase of savings, since suppliers had strong incentives to be ranked first. Given the strategy adopted, the framework agreement is a real success, particularly as there has been no supply disruption.

Note

1. Case study submitted by the French central purchasing body UGAP (*Union des groupements d'achats publics*).

Annex D.

Italy: Call for tender structure

Context

Founded in 1997, Consip is the Italian central purchasing body, it is 100% owned by the Ministry of Economy and Finance (MEF). Since 2000, Consip has been tasked with the implementation of the Programme for the Rationalisation of Public Spending on Goods and Services, which includes the use of tools such as framework agreements. Energy is one of the product/service categories that Consip provides to public administrations. In 2005, Consip's energy unit realised, by means of analysis and market research, that there was room for designing a framework agreement, for the first time, in the procurement of heating services. This area absorbed 34% of the national energy expenditure (about EUR 3.4 billion annually) and accounted for approximately 5% of the Italian energy market. The expected target was to achieve economical savings of 5-10% and equivalent energy savings.

Consip issued the first edition of the Integrated Energy Service tender in 2006, and further developed services provided under this umbrella, which now includes the provision of electrical systems. The framework agreement is now running under the third edition, and the fourth edition notice has been recently published.

Objectives

The key objective of the framework agreement was to provide services for the largest possible number of administrations disseminated throughout the country, while ensuring sufficient flexibility as it was not possible to list the buildings to be heated and their technical/physical features.

Taking into account the strong environmental considerations, another objective of the framework agreement was to ensure that it was a performance-based approach that would achieve shared savings. The suppliers would be paid for a fixed flat rate, and then further compensated once the energy performance target has been achieved.

Consip's final objective was to gradually increase environmental performance targets, as well as sustainable market development. New framework agreements are therefore now referred to as "Total Energy Building Framework Agreements".

Implementation

Before the issuance of each tender edition, Consip undertook a market analysis based on historical data and information deriving from the answers provided by suppliers to questionnaires published on Consip's website, as well as public announcements of companies' schedules and scope of forthcoming procurement initiatives. Online questionnaires included information about the geographical coverage of the companies and reasons that would prevent companies from bidding.

Prior to the first edition, Consip thoroughly analysed the needs and capacity of contracting authorities and suppliers. Despite the interest shown by major stakeholders, investments in energy efficiency were not developing due to several barriers:

- Absence of specific standards (measures, benchmarking, procedures, etc.) and low awareness of existing opportunities of energy efficiencies in public buildings.
- Lack of expertise among public employees to partner with the industry.

To overcome these challenges, Consip included in the tender documentation the identification of a technical person for each contracting authority that suppliers should commit to train on energy efficiency themes. Informative meetings on the subject have also been organised that aim to raise awareness of the topic and promote the use of a framework agreement strategy that enables economies of scale and a decrease of administrative costs.

To analyse the supply side, several meetings took place with the main trade associations and with all energy service companies (ESCOs) that had won in previous relevant tenders to discuss the critical aspects that emerged during the execution of the previous relevant contracts. This meant that suppliers were involved before the decision of a tendering strategy and were offered the opportunity to present their views, so that the best strategy could be chosen by Consip.

Considering the inherent coverage uncertainty in terms of buildings, Consip decided to design the first tender with the view of implementing a framework agreement open to all public administrations. Therefore, the tendering process was developed starting from a business case on a specific public building that was extrapolated to the entire value of the tender and number of forecasted buildings. The following editions thus benefited from a refined assessment of the contract coverage.

Table A.D.1. Coverage of the framework agreement

Tender edition	Number of contracting authorities	Contract value (Million EUR)	Number of buildings
1	324	803	5.800
2	298	1.367	7.200

Note: Results of the 3rd edition are not available yet

Impact and monitoring

The tendering process has always been an open procedure on the basis of the most economically advantageous tender (MEAT), whereby 60% was allocated to price and 40% to quality. Considering previous market analyses and to best develop the capacity of the supply base in the local areas, each tender has been divided into 12 geographical lots aimed at increasing competition and fostering the participation of small and medium-sized enterprises.

Table A.D.2. Suppliers participating in the calls for tenders

Tender edition	Number of participating ESCOs	% of ESCO SMEs	Number of ESCO winners	% ESCO SME winners
1	34	50%	13	15%
2	58	67%	32	75%
3	65	62%	n/a	n/a

Note: Results of the 3rd edition are only partial

In order to reduce energy consumption at the national level, Consip adopted a strategy based on energy performance contracts. The basic idea is that the supplier of the energy service should be motivated and encouraged to optimise energy consumption and resource management to improve their profitability.

Award criteria were aimed at encouraging suppliers to reduce primary energy consumption and the associated CO_2 emissions of the entire building/heating plant system by measures such as substitution of hot water heating, insulation, and renewable thermal sources.

In the first two editions of the framework agreement, energy efficiency results were certified by the Italian Electrical Energy and Gas Authority. In the third edition, ESCOs were asked to implement a measure and verification system of energy consumption and savings. This element was part of the awarding criteria.

An average of 25% of cost savings for public administrations was achieved involving approximately 13 000 buildings. Contracts for the first two editions executed had a total (estimated) financial value of EUR 2.216 million.

Challenges and risks

Considering the structure of the tender, one of the main challenges was to ensure sufficient competition in all regional lots. The extent and duration of the market consultation phase helped minimise the risk of there being no proposal for one lot. On average, more than 50 ESCOs participated in each tender edition, and around 50% of ESCO winners were SMEs.

The novelty of the procurement strategy, and notably the performance-based technical specifications aimed at fostering innovation, posed a significant challenge. This approach, while incentivising suppliers' creativity, creates an additional risk of receiving proposals that do not meet the technical criteria. Asking for suppliers' feedback on the draft technical specifications helped to minimise this risk. All suppliers involved were able to comply with the technical criteria requested, and there was enhanced competition on the technical features included in the tender.

Key lessons learned

The pre-procurement market consultation was one of the most important parts of the procurement process, and was carried out using online questionnaires for suppliers, in addition to meetings with suppliers. The duration of this phase in the first edition took about two years to be completed in accordance with the complexity of the project and the novelty of the tender structure. It then progressively reduced in subsequent editions as a result of information previously collected.

Thorough market investigation provided Consip with a greater understanding of the structure and appetite of the supply side, which enhanced competition in the call for tender phase.

Considering the nature of the contractual relationship between Consip and the awarded suppliers with performance-based framework agreements, the duration of the contract has been identified as a crucial factor in ensuring sustainable relationships. Since suppliers are only compensated once the energy performance is being reached, the duration of the agreement has an immediate impact on the suppliers' return on investment.

The principle environmental impacts are related to CO_2 emissions caused by energy consumption. In order to reduce these impacts, the contracts included a performance clause requiring a minimum amount of energy to be saved measured in tonnes of oil equivalent (TOE). This minimum threshold has been significantly exceeded.

Cumulatively, these framework agreements resulted in almost 78 000 TOE saved, translating into EUR 62 million. It enabled the avoidance of 200 000 tonnes of CO_2 emissions.

In addition, the framework agreements helped standardise the energy service procurement process across the country, since almost 630 contracting authorities have had recourse to the same procurement instrument for a total contract value of EUR 2 216 million.

The success of this framework contract has helped Italian public authorities to lead by example in energy savings regarding citizens and the private sector, as they have complied with their procurement obligations and with the Directives 2006/32/EC and 2012/27/UE on energy end-use efficiency and energy services.

The last edition of this framework agreement won the European Energy Service Award in 2014, and was among the five finalists at the Procurement of Innovation Award 2015.

Annex E.

New Zealand: Procurement capability index

Context

In 2012, the New Zealand Government introduced the Procurement Functional Leadership (PFL) programme to build on initiatives and momentum gained from the preceding procurement reform programme. PFL places a greater focus on building procurement effectiveness across the public sector. The Chief Executive of the Ministry of Business, Innovation and Employment was appointed Procurement Functional Leader to:

- Provide stronger leadership across government procurement activities.
- Accelerate the improvement of state services' commercial acumen, procurement capability and capacity.
- Deliver better procurement results for government, leading to better services and value for money.

The October 2012 cabinet paper, Government Procurement Functional Leadership, stated that: "commercial capability building is the number one priority for the PFL" and that actions should: "…stimulate procurement capability building, develop and implement a procurement maturity index to measure and track procurement performance of all State Services agencies…and report results to Cabinet on an annual basis".

The resulting Procurement Capability Index (PCI) is a priority project for the New Zealand Government Procurement agency (NZGP). The PCI was developed and piloted in 2015, and will be rolled out to agencies in 2016/17.

Objectives

The PCI is a self-assessment tool that government agencies can use to measure and track their commercial skills, develop improvement plans, and benchmark their performance against other agencies. It poses a range of questions linked to a rating system that are used to evaluate an agency's commercial capability against a scale of strong, well-placed, needing development, or weak.

The PCI is designed to work in harmony with other central New Zealand government agencies, such as the Treasury and the State Services Commission, to jointly drive improved commercial practices. PCI results will help to inform and assist the Treasury with investment decision making. It will also inform senior leadership performance evaluations conducted by the State Services Commission.

Implementation

Agencies will be required to annually complete and submit a PCI assessment and provide supporting metrics. The results will be reported to cabinet ministers and published on the NZGP website. The assessment is based on a capability maturity model that consists of 42 questions covering 11 categories, which are:

1. Strategy and outcomes: Strategic planning for commercial outcomes
2. Strategy and outcomes: Procurement strategy alignment with agency key result areas
3. Commercial leadership: Commercial leadership to drive outcomes
4. Stakeholder engagement: Procurement function engagement with stakeholders
5. Governance: Governance and organisation of the procurement function
6. Policy and practice: Alignment with policy and processes
7. Suppliers and providers: Sourcing and collaboration
8. Supplier and provider relationships: Supplier relationship management
9. People: Management of people and skills development
10. People: Knowledge and performance management
11. Technology: Use of technology processes and tools

The PCI self-assessment will be supported by review and moderation processes to ensure confidence in the results and to drive consistency across the agencies. The moderation process allows for a mix of supplier and provider feedback, and peer and external reviews.

Impact and Monitoring

The PCI concept is focused on promoting improvements in commercial skills and procurement capability over time. Performance improvement is expected to happen as insights gained through the self-assessment process are captured, discussed and acted on within and across agencies. In other cases, insights will come from the reflections of an advisory group, who will look across the results of all agencies. The insights will help agencies focus their collective efforts on improving commercial expertise and procurement effectiveness.

For each agency, a report will be produced that summarises the key issues, opportunities and impacts identified for that agency. An executive summary of the agency's results will also be produced and published on the NZGP website, along with an overview report that identifies findings that impact multiple agencies.

Challenges and risks

There is a risk of inconsistency in results given the variance in commercial capability across the 100+ agencies that will participate in the programme. This will be managed using a mix of peer reviewers and oversight from an advisory group made up of chief procurement officers from a range of agencies. Where agency scoring is either high or low, external experts will be engaged to review the evidence used to support the agency's self-assessment. Such reviews will include:

- Interview with the Tier 3 procurement manager
- Spot checks of the agency's supporting evidence
- Assessment of the level of confidence in the agency's evidence.

Another major risk involves establishing credibility in the eyes of both suppliers and the public in general. It would be easy for the integrity of the PCI review and moderation process to be damaged if assessments were deemed to be a case of government agencies rating themselves too highly without good reason.

To mitigate this, the PCI process allows for supplier feedback from a range of sources, including:

- Industry groups, such as business reference groups and social sector umbrella groups
- Compliments and complaints from suppliers and providers
- Supplier and provider feedback gained through reviews and surveys
- Annual surveys undertaken by NZGP

Key lessons learned

The views of stakeholders are critical in establishing an evaluation programme with integrity. Review and moderation processes in particular must be able to stand up to scrutiny if the programme is to have the credibility to be taken seriously by the public, suppliers and government leaders.

Annex F.

United Kingdom: Stakeholder involvement in tender design

Background

The Crown commercial service (CCS) is an executive agency, sponsored by the Cabinet Office, that manages the procurement of common goods and services and leads on procurement policy on behalf of the UK government. The CCS used communication and its website to ensure the early engagement of suppliers and contracting authorities.

Implementation and process

To engage suppliers and contracting authorities it is important to publish online accessible information on the procurement pipeline that everyone can find easily:

- Procurement recently awarded and underway

Information available covers the category of products and services, the name of the agreement and its code and its starting date Providing information on recently awarded procurement is important for suppliers who were not aware of this procurement opportunity as they will have an idea of when the next framework agreement will be planned.

- Planned procurement

Information available covers the category of products and services, the name of the agreement and the planned publication date in the OJEU (the Official Journal of the European Union), and the planned award date.

- Future procurement under consideration

Information available covers the category of products and services and the name of the agreement.

Concerning planned procurement, for some framework agreements it is also possible to access the following through the CCS website:

- The pre-information notice
- The project timescales
- Documentation such as:
  - Draft statement of requirement
  - Draft specification
  - Draft allotment strategy under consideration
  - Draft pricing strategies

- Custumer and supplier engagement activities (separately)
  - Meetings
  - Webinars
  - Questionnaires
  - Workshops
  - Seminars

Key lessons learned

For contracting authorities, these activities represent a real opportunity to provide feedback on different draft documentation at least a few months before the expected tender publication date. For suppliers, it is an occasion to discuss the draft documentation related to the framework agreement and get answers to any questions they may have in a confidential environment.

The early engagement of suppliers and contracting authorities through different means enables a better design of the tender specification, thereby matching contracting authority needs and the products and services available in the market.

Further information

Further information can be found at: http://ccs-agreements.cabinetoffice.gov.uk /project-management-and-full-design-team-services-rm3741.

Annex G.

United States: Guidance on framework agreements

Context

The US General Services Administration (GSA) provides centralised procurement for the federal government. With a budget of USD 23.9 billion, financed at 99% from services provided to federal agencies, GSA employed 11 495 full-time staff as of June 2014. GSA is composed of four main services:

- **Federal Acquisition Service (FAS),** which provides multiple contracting vehicles, fleet management, travel and transportation management, and government-wide purchase card services to all Federal agencies and other entities of the US Government.
- **Public Building Service (PBS)**, the landlord for the civilian Federal Government. It acquires space on behalf of the Federal Government through new construction and leasing, and acts as a caretaker for Federal properties across the country.
- **Office of Government-wide Policy (OGP)** the policy-making authority covering the areas of personal and real property, travel and transportation, information technology, regulatory information and use of Federal advisory committees.
- **Office of Citizen Services & Innovative Technologies (OCSIT)**, the nation's focal point for data, information and services offered by the Federal Government to citizens.

FAS is responsible for implementing and managing the Multiple Award Schedules (MAS) in accordance with the Federal Acquisition Regulation (FAR). The MAS programme provides eligible ordering activities, with a simplified process for obtaining supplies and services. Schedule contracts are multiple award, indefinite delivery and indefinite quantity (IDIQ) contracts, which are awarded to responsible companies that offer commercial supplies or services at prices determined to be fair and reasonable at the GSA/base contract level. Contracts are awarded as IDIQ five-year contracts with three five-year options. GSA/FAS awards and administers these IDIQ contracts, but allows qualified users to access them as their own. Products and services are ordered directly from schedule contractors.

The MAS programme provides purchasing entities with more than 40 million commercial supplies (products) and services at volume discount pricing through 39 open and standing solicitations (including 9 managed by the Department of Veteran Affairs for medical supplies and services).

Objectives

The overarching objective of the MAS programme is to foster cost savings for US Federal contracting authorities, while ensuring compliance with procurement regulations. To this end, the MAS programme provides the following features:

- Up-to-date, FAR-compliant acquisition vehicles that help minimise risks.
- Competitive market-based pricing that leverages the buying power of the federal government, with the ability to negotiate further discounts at the order level.
- Acquisition experts available to help customers make the most of MAS.
- On-site and online training for help in using and maximising the benefits of using MAS.

Assistance and support provided by FAS directly contribute to achieving the main objective of this programme: cost savings based on volume discounts pricing and reducing red tape costs by not requiring the Federal Agency to create a stand-alone contract vehicle.

Implementation

FAS has developed comprehensive guidance in various formats that go beyond the mere operational use of the MAS programme. A revisited dedicated MAS portal was implemented in early 2011 and provides a one-stop shop for resources and assistance with using the schedules.

The portal offers a central location for contracting authorities to access all of the resources and tools available online. Improved features include video and audio training, a searchable MAS Desk Reference Guide, and access to the MAS blog and discussion forums in Interact, the FAS social media platform and online community. Regularly updated training programmes based on the core competencies of the GS-1102 Contracting Series help contracting authorities easily navigate the schedules and learn how to implement FAR compliant ordering processes.

This series of training materials target different audiences, from federal entities, state and local governments, to vendors and students. Some training activities also offer the possibility to earn continuous learning points (CLPs) that may count towards contracting certification and continuing education, which are required for continued certification. Participants learn how to effectively use the schedules programme to meet their requirements, use tools to enhance competition, achieve small business utilisation, or procure sustainable acquisitions.

The MAS portal also incorporates enhanced tools and resources for suppliers, including a revamped Vendor Support Center. The Vendor Support Center provides an entry point for both GSA schedule and government-wide acquisition contract holders to access resources designed to help them work with FAS and federal, state, and local contracting authorities.

The guides notably include sections on:

- The different objectives of the MAS programme.
- The lists of supplies and services that can be procured through MAS.

- Whether the use of MAS is the best procurement route.
- Acquisition strategies using MAS.
- Acquisition flexibilities in using MAS, such as the grouping of needs under Blanket Purchase Agreements (BPAs), and possibilities for contracting authorities to request Contractor Team Arrangements (CTAs) that enable two or more vendors to present a team approach to providing solutions, which is different from a prime contractor/subcontractor relationship.

In addition to training materials, contracting authorities and the general public have access to detailed information about the performance of MAS when entering the dedicated platform. This information provides buyers with insights into how a specific MAS is distributed across suppliers, the socio-economic distribution of suppliers, and the performance of MAS as an economic catalyst against geographical areas.

Impact and monitoring

The FAS Office of Acquisition Management, Training Division was officially established towards the end of 2015. Previously, the Office of Acquisition Management had operated a robust training programme under the auspices of the Office's Policy Division. The creation of the separate division has resulted in a significant increase in the number of in person training activities conducted during the first quarter of 2016, which has equalled the total number of training activities (21) conducted in 2015. The Division is currently working on expanding its online and on demand offerings, with the expectation that similar increases in the number of participants will be realised in these mediums. In addition, during the Spring of 2016, the Division inaugurated the first National Trainer cohort. These individuals will receive training on the existing curriculum, as well as specialised training to address adult learning methodologies and course/curriculum development. National Trainers will, on a collateral basis, be assigned to conduct acquisition training throughout the United States, with a focus on the geographic regions within which they reside.

Challenges and risks

As a division that is developing programmes new to GSA and FAS, it is still working to develop baselines for future resource needs. The Division believes that as the programme and capacity to offer training increases, so too will the need for additional resources. However, it has intentionally chosen to pursue a path that maximises existing talent within FAS on a collateral basis. One major risk is that it could result in an increase in capacity that is disproportionate to the resources required.

Key lessons learned

The MAS programme has the potential to drive various efficiencies in terms of processing costs, simplification of the procurement process and savings, however, it is also a complex system considering the wide array of products and services available and the number of suppliers enrolled.

The move away from standardised goods and services, and the integration of more complex offerings, generates additional challenges. Audits carried out by the GSA Office of Inspector General suggest that most of the irregularities found in the processing of orders related to less standardised purchases, notably to the procurement of complex services.

Providing detailed guidance on how procurement tools such as MAS could yield various benefits for the contracting authorities is a major step towards procurement efficiency. Not only has it helped end-users to navigate the MAS programme, it has also offered FAS the opportunity to convey key messages to a public procurement audience, and instil a culture of effectiveness and efficiency in using the MAS programme.

ORGANISATION FOR ECONOMIC CO-OPERATION AND DEVELOPMENT

The OECD is a unique forum where governments work together to address the economic, social and environmental challenges of globalisation. The OECD is also at the forefront of efforts to understand and to help governments respond to new developments and concerns, such as corporate governance, the information economy and the challenges of an ageing population. The Organisation provides a setting where governments can compare policy experiences, seek answers to common problems, identify good practice and work to co-ordinate domestic and international policies.

The OECD member countries are: Australia, Austria, Belgium, Canada, Chile, the Czech Republic, Denmark, Estonia, Finland, France, Germany, Greece, Hungary, Iceland, Ireland, Israel, Italy, Japan, Korea, Latvia, Luxembourg, Mexico, the Netherlands, New Zealand, Norway, Poland, Portugal, the Slovak Republic, Slovenia, Spain, Sweden, Switzerland, Turkey, the United Kingdom and the United States. The European Union takes part in the work of the OECD.

OECD Publishing disseminates widely the results of the Organisation's statistics gathering and research on economic, social and environmental issues, as well as the conventions, guidelines and standards agreed by its members.

OECD PUBLISHING, 2, rue André-Pascal, 75775 PARIS CEDEX 16
(42 2017 25 1 P) ISBN 978-92-64-27517-1 – 2017

www.ingramcontent.com/pod-product-compliance
Lightning Source LLC
LaVergne TN
LVHW081410110826
845149LV00010B/1686

9789264275171